BECOMING A
CRITICAL THINKER

BECOMING
A CRITICAL
THINKER

A WORKBOOK TO HELP STUDENTS THINK WELL IN AN AGE OF DISINFORMATION

JULIE BOGART

A TARCHERPERIGEE BOOK

tarcherperigee

an imprint of Penguin Random House LLC
penguinrandomhouse.com

Most TarcherPerigee books are available at special quantity discounts for bulk purchase for sales promotions, premiums, fund-raising, and educational needs. Special books or book excerpts also can be created to fit specific needs. For details, write: SpecialMarkets@penguinrandomhouse.com.

Trade paperback ISBN: 9780593712818

Printed in the United States of America
1st Printing

Book design by Shannon Nicole Plunkett

CONTENTS

Part Three

THE APPLICATION: LEARNING THE ART OF INTERPRETATION

PREFACE

You're smarter than many adults think you are. Every day, grown-ups tell you what they believe you should think, do, be, and say. They want to guide you past the mistakes they made when they were your age. The irony is, those adults made their own judgments at the time and learned from those decisions—the same way you make decisions for yourself right now and are learning, too! You may be worried that I, like so many others, am about to tell you what to think—I'm not. I'm here to help you see and understand your *own* thinking.

The genius of your mind is that you have access to data, experiences, facts, and clues to help you make the decisions you make. You forge ahead, deciding what course of action to take or what belief to hold or what opinion to express. You risk sharing the outcome of all that thinking, and then adults in your life—your parents or teachers or relatives or coaches—express their opinions about that thinking. You may wonder why they ignore the important pieces of information that you used to make the call you made. It may feel like they treat your thoughts and ideas as ill-informed or insufficient. To protect you, they may set up guidelines and enforce them using their authority in your life as the primary criteria for overriding what you know in your gut was the right course of action for you.

Think about all the times you believed that it was in your best interest to play a video game for longer than your parents believed was good for you, or a time when you shared a belief that you were told was too idealistic. In those moments, you may have experienced an insult to your intelligence and a feeling that the factors that matter to you are being dismissed. The disregard of your beliefs, ideas, thoughts, and experiences can lead to resentment and an unwillingness to learn from others—

particularly parents or teachers. I get it! I've lived it, too. I have the diaries full of resentment against the adults in my life to prove it.

To be fair, sometimes any one of us doesn't have enough data to make the best call, and yet we make one anyway. We may not know there is more information we should consider, or we willfully ignore what we know matters because some other idea trumps its importance. Sometimes we're misled by misinformation or deceit. More experience and data are often needed to ensure safety or the best outcome. On the other hand, every single one of your choices can be traced back to what felt utterly logical to you at the time! If asked to reflect, I bet you can identify the bits and pieces of experience, research, information, relationship, and context that account for the choices you make and the beliefs you hold. What's infuriating is to be held accountable for *more* than that, right? Most of us want someone to at least tell us, "From where you sit with what you know, your choice does make sense."

We want that understanding, even for those decisions that, upon reflection, seem entirely boneheaded—like speeding in your car to beat curfew and winding up in a wreck. There's a reason you stayed too long at your friend's house, and there's a reason you felt that angering your parents was more risky than speeding in your car, and there's a reason you took that turn too quickly and your body didn't react fast enough to avoid crashing into the tree. Each of those reasons is reasonable (in other words, each makes some kind of sense) when viewed from the totality of your choices, your thoughts, the information you knew, your relationships, and your prior experiences.

When we talk about critical thinking, then, it's not just the ability to explain why your parents' curfew was a bad idea to begin with. Rather, it's the capacity to pivot to your own internal world—the thought life that lives inside you. It's the ability to make visible the countless factors that inform why you see the world the way you do—and then to hold as equally valuable the fact that everyone else is doing *exactly the same thing* every time they present you with their righter-than-rain perspectives.

In this workbook, I have an agenda. I'd like to be up-front about it. In my adult life, I have revised my many beliefs more times than it takes to beat *Mario Kart*, which, according to data I just googled, takes about fifty hours of dedicated play. Applied to my mind, that's fifty hours of dedicated thinking about any given thought during each season of my life. That's a lot of thinking! As I learned how to gather the data, information, facts, and experiences I needed to think well, I grew into a more and more skillful thinker (imagine that!).

The thing is, you're thinking that much, too! That's the nature of thinking—you do it all the time, and frankly, you do it really well. My first objective is to show you just how well you use your mind already. What we want to do in this workbook, as you try the activities and consider the ideas I offer, is to increase your capacity to include more thoughts, more perspectives, and more insight! How will you identify misinformation in ChatGPT (the artificial intelligence platform that generates writing) or recognize when you're being manipulated by a leader in your community? What skills help you discover what's true? Your thinking creates the life you lead and the world we all share. Your thinking will be the key to how your generation and those following think and reason. It might be a staggering idea, but truly, you and your friends will one day run the world! Let's get ready to do it well now.

This book provides a set of tools, processes, and journal prompts that will help you design a life you love—one that fulfills you, promotes great relationships, and contributes to the advancement of humankind! Tall order? I think you're up to it! Pop in your earbuds, open a streaming app, and listen to some good music while you work through this book.

INTRODUCTION

Are you ready to rock your world? The lessons in this workbook will absolutely alter how you think about thinking. Even some of your thoughts will change. The most important advice I can give you as you get started is this: **any belief you examine or any ideal you reconsider can be changed back to the one that feels safest to you.** We're playing here, not requiring lifelong commitments to new thoughts. The only risk you take is to do the exercise and see where it leads. Enter this work with a spirit of curiosity and play, not tightfisted allegiances. You're in charge of your mind. No one else! You get to think private and new thoughts, to question habits of thought, and even to rethink those new ideas. You have the right to know what you think and why. You also have the right to change your mind!

All of it takes courage. The more tools you have to think well, the easier it gets. This workbook is intended to help you do the following:

- Understand critical thinking

- Develop habits of practice that aid you in thinking well

- Imagine how other people think

- Expand your thinking through reading, experiences, and encounters

- Generate insight into thorny issues (broadscale or personal)

- Become comfortable with dissent and difference of opinion

- Discover how to interpret the thoughts of others

HOW TO USE THIS WORKBOOK

This workbook is divided into three parts:

1. The Foundation: Understanding Critical Thinking

2. The Practice: Growing Your Thinking Skills

3. The Application: Learning the Art of Interpretation

Work through each section at your own pace. Each part contains several lessons, and I've divided each lesson into three parts: a brief, an activity, and a journal prompt. I've also indicated when the activity bears repeating! Some activities are meant for a singular "aha" experience. Others help you develop skills that require practice.

THE LESSONS

— Briefs

Each lesson starts with a "brief"—a quick take on the kind of thinking needed for the activity or process that follows. Read the brief. It will give you the overarching principle that the activity is meant to teach. Notice resistance, smugness, a surge of adrenaline, or any other "thinking tell" you might have as you read about the concepts. A thinking tell is a felt experience or reaction to what you read. (Part One, Lesson One: The Academic Selfie teaches you how to identify thinking tells.) When you find something dull or provocative, note that. When you feel swept up by fervor or agreement, note that, too! These are ways your mind copes with and interprets new ideas. Noticing the thinking tell helps neutralize its effect. You don't have to do anything but notice and keep reading. Jot down margin notes—they're so helpful! Let the briefs give you a frame of reference for the activities that follow.

— Activities

After you've read the brief, set aside some time to do the activity. Each one will take anywhere between ten and forty-five minutes, although you may want to take longer, and that is wonderful! Completing one or two activities per week is plenty. I'll indicate which activities benefit from repetition and practice. Each activity is designed to give a direct experience of how to shift your thinking or how to conduct research.

My book *Raising Critical Thinkers* goes into more depth about the underlying concepts. If you're interested, you can always turn to that book for a deeper dive into the ideas. That said, reading the original book is not necessary. Doing the activities will deliver a direct experience of the thinking tool. You'll learn through experience and encounter, rather than merely through reading.

— Journal

At the end of each activity, you'll find a prompt to help you reflect on your thinking and how it changed or didn't. By the end of the workbook, you'll have a record that shows the development of how you process inputs and what you do to expand the possible ways to think about any idea or experience. Pretty cool, huh? You can write right in the workbook! Pick a pen you like. It helps.

THE FOUNDATION: UNDERSTANDING CRITICAL THINKING

THE ACADEMIC SELFIE

Noticing Your "Thinking Tells"

(WORTH REPEATING)

BRIEF

To become a critical thinker, you don't start with the "other guy's thinking" but instead with your own. Picture your cell phone. You want to take a photo of yourself so you flip the camera lens around so you can see yourself. In that moment, you may push a strand of hair behind your ear or practice a smile or smirk. You experiment with an angle to bring in the most light, or you adjust the distance you hold the phone from your face—maybe even propping it on a counter and setting a timer to get a little distance from the lens. You do all of this by considering the factors that help you get the best look, the best angle, the best frame for your face.

The academic selfie is a similar strategy for your mind. You're going to flip the camera around to examine your own thinking before examining someone else's. You'll notice what's out of place, how your views look to you, and how they might be seen by others. You might readjust the angle of how you research or how you understand a critique of a strongly held belief. Ultimately, you pay attention to how your mind engages with the subject matter first, before you examine how other people see the same topic.

Because we live inside our own bodies and think thoughts in our minds, it's easy to lose touch with how we make meaning and judgments. We consult a personal feeling of "rightness," or how what we choose to believe lines up with what we've learned at home, in school, online, on TV, or via radio. We compare what we think with what we've been taught in our religious communities. We think about where we live or how we are being raised. One of the ways to make your own viewpoint visible is to ask yourself this question: "What do I hope will be true?" That little question does a great job of helping you flip the camera around for self-examination.

So where do you begin? Let's look at the invisible reactions you might experience as you read or digest new information. I call these body experiences and feelings "thinking tells." They're the automatic responses you have when you encounter any data or idea. Defensiveness is one of the most common thinking tells. It means someone is inching too near a cherished belief.

ACTIVITY

STEP ONE: Let's discover your habits of reaction to new information—your thinking tells. On a scale of 1 to 10, how likely are you to be influenced by the following factors when you take in new information?

- I feel defensive when someone criticizes a view I hold dearly.

  ○ ○ ○ ○ ○ ○ ○ ○ ○ ○
  1 2 3 4 5 6 7 8 9 10

- I feel smug when I read an argument I have already discredited.

  ○ ○ ○ ○ ○ ○ ○ ○ ○ ○
  1 2 3 4 5 6 7 8 9 10

- I go blank when I have to process or remember numbers and statistics.

  ○ ○ ○ ○ ○ ○ ○ ○ ○ ○
  1 2 3 4 5 6 7 8 9 10

- I feel persuaded by scientific research and data.

  ○ ○ ○ ○ ○ ○ ○ ○ ○ ○
  1 2 3 4 5 6 7 8 9 10

- I feel annoyed when I hear a fact I don't want to be true.

  ○ ○ ○ ○ ○ ○ ○ ○ ○ ○
  1 2 3 4 5 6 7 8 9 10

- I give less credence to the topic if the writing is dull.

  O O O O O O O O O O
  1 2 3 4 5 6 7 8 9 10

- I'm suspicious of the writing if it is passionate and emotional.

  O O O O O O O O O O
  1 2 3 4 5 6 7 8 9 10

- I prefer writing that leans more toward personal experience than objective facts.

  O O O O O O O O O O
  1 2 3 4 5 6 7 8 9 10

- I trust writing that leans more toward objective facts than personal experience.

  O O O O O O O O O O
  1 2 3 4 5 6 7 8 9 10

- I favor a writer who is from a similar background to mine.

  O O O O O O O O O O
  1 2 3 4 5 6 7 8 9 10

- I'm suspicious of a writer who is from a background very different from mine.

  O O O O O O O O O O
  1 2 3 4 5 6 7 8 9 10

- I automatically exclude information that doesn't match what I expect to be true.

  O O O O O O O O O O
  1 2 3 4 5 6 7 8 9 10

- When an idea makes me nervous, it's because I'm wondering, "What would my [parent, spiritual leader, best friend, teacher] say about it?"

  O O O O O O O O O O
  1 2 3 4 5 6 7 8 9 10

Next, identify any of the thinking tells that you rated 6 or above on the scale. As you process new information, these tells are the invisible, subtle influences on your thinking. They exert a lot of pressure on how you make meaning with your mind. Make a list of them here.

_____

_____

_____

_____

_____

STEP TWO: Show your tells! Practice noticing and letting go of your thinking tells by engaging with controversial topics.

Make a list of controversial topics—topics that have strong proponents on both sides. This could be a personal issue, like whether or not to go to college, or a social issue, like whether or not the drinking age should be lowered.

_____

_____

_____

_____

_____

1. Select two topics.

2. Conduct an online search to find articles about the topics. Read two articles that represent opposing views for each topic.

3. Identify your "lean" before you read the articles. Do you lean pro or con?

4. List the thinking tells you experience as you read each side of the argument. You might include some tells that were not on the earlier list. That's perfect!

TOPIC	ARTICLE TITLE AND SOURCE

TOPIC	ARTICLE TITLE AND SOURCE

TOPIC	ARTICLE TITLE AND SOURCE

TOPIC	ARTICLE TITLE AND SOURCE

JOURNAL

When I don't like what I'm reading or hearing, my body reacts—it buzzes with electricity, my stomach gets upset, my jaw clenches, and my face feels hot. Write what your body does:

In the writing space that follows, answer any of these questions:

- What did you learn about yourself?

- How willing are you to read what doesn't match what you want to be true?

- How triggered were you by the view you don't hold?

- How smug did you feel reading the view you hold?

- What else did you notice about your reactions when you read provocative information?

This exercise helps you see how reactive you were when reading these articles. You can use this tool anytime you read an article or hear information that provokes a strong bodily or emotional response. Notice the thinking tell, and rate it! The more you become self-aware, the easier it is to set aside the impact of that thinking tell to consider the challenging information.

_____

_____

_____

_____

_____

_____

_____

PART ONE: THE FOUNDATION

SAYS WHO?

Identifying the Storyteller

(ONE TIME)

BRIEF

Any topic worthy of debate comes to us funneled through a human being—a person, just like you. No matter how carefully a writer or speaker, like a scientist or an academic researcher, attempts to present an objective view of a topic, even the choice to include or exclude information shapes how you receive it. Objectivity is an illusion, even though reducing subjectivity is a worthy goal in particular types of writing. To be a skillful critical thinker means identifying the viewpoint of the person presenting the story or information. Once that's identified, you can ask some questions to help you recognize the implicit bias. By the way, having a bias is inherent to being human. It's not bad or wrong. It just is. It's also worth noticing!

ACTIVITY

Let's play with viewpoints in fairy tales. You will need to check out the book *The True Story of the 3 Little Pigs* by Jon Scieszka from your local library. You'll use the book as a reference later in this exercise.

First, retell the story of "The Three Little Pigs" as you are most familiar with it. Conduct an online search, and read several versions of the story. Focus on the viewpoint of the storyteller. Answer the following questions for any of the versions you selected:

- Who is telling the story?

  _____

- Who is the hero, and who is the villain, according to this version of the story? (There may be more than one of each, depending on the version.)

  _____

  _____

- What justification is given for blowing down the pigs' houses?

  _____

  _____

  _____

- What is the moral guideline that the story upholds?

  _____

  _____

  _____

- What conclusion is the reader meant to draw about who is to blame? How do you know?

  _____

  _____

_____

_____

In the above retelling, you're likely to have come across an "omniscient narrator"—a storyteller who appears unbiased but has access to the motivations of all the characters in the story. We've been trained to see this viewpoint as "objective," or as divorced from bias. Yet as you just identified, as a reader, you learned who to root for and who to root against, who to feel sympathy toward and who to blame. How objective can that narrator be when you're being guided to adopt a perspective about the pigs and the wolf as you read the story? On what basis are you siding with the pigs and against the wolf in these traditional versions of the tale?

Now read *The True Story of the 3 Little Pigs* by Jon Scieszka. Answer these questions again:

- Who is telling the story this time?

_____

- Who is the hero, and who is the villain, according to this version of the story?

_____

_____

- What justification is given for blowing down the pigs' houses?

_____

_____

_____

- What is the moral guideline that the story upholds?

_____

_____

_____

- What conclusion is the reader meant to draw about who is to blame? How do you know?

_____

_____

_____

_____

According to the cover of the picture book, this time the story is told by "A. Wolf." In this retelling of the fairy tale, the reader is introduced to a different point of view. We're being invited to consider that the wolf was perhaps not accurately represented in the original story. Each storyteller has an agenda. In the original story of the three little pigs, the narrator appeals to our well-established sense of law and order. We align with the narrator because of a number of factors, including the following:

- How many times we've heard the story

- The belief that wolves are dangerous (a bias cultivated through lots of fairy tales that include wolves as villains)

- The idea that a homeowner deserves to be safe in their own home

- The fact that blowing down a house and eating the pigs (in some versions) constitutes breaking the law

- The habit of receiving our news from an impersonal voice, not a participant in the story

In literature, there's a literary device called the "unreliable narrator." Stories told through the perspective of an unreliable narrator share a common thread: the storyteller is usually mounting a defense for "crimes" or "misdeeds." In the case of A. Wolf, whether or not we agree with his defense, we have a chance to picture how a wolf might justify his actions. Storytellers control the flavor of the information they share. It's up to us to name that storyteller and identify their agenda.

JOURNAL

Think of a favorite story (a fairy tale or movie series like *Star Wars* or any Marvel or DC Comics film, for example). Retell the story from the villain's perspective. You can make up excuses for the villain, but try to contextualize the choices the villain makes to support their goals and the story. For instance, how would you tell the story of *Star Wars* from Darth Vader's perspective and make it sympathetic to his choices? You might try telling the same story from a bystander's viewpoint as well. Ask yourself how much more you need to know in order to create a believable storyline for why that character acted in particular ways.

The goal, by the way, is understanding, not sympathy. You can still disapprove of someone's decisions or actions while understanding how they came to make those decisions or take those actions.

FAB VOCAB
QUICK-WRITE

Defining Your Terms

(WORTH REPEATING)

BRIEF

One of the most important aspects of thinking well is being aware of how you define terms that recur in the field of study. When we begin a research project or listen to a news or sports broadcast, we're swayed by our own definitions of terms. For instance, consider the word "obsessed." Maybe you hear this word and think "addiction" or "compulsion." You might see being obsessed as unhealthy or needing treatment. Someone else may assume it means the person is an überfan—someone who devotes their loyalty and enthusiasm to a musical artist or celebrity. Someone else might hear the word "obsessed" and think of the word "love"—that this person is head over heels for another person or a personal passion, as in, "I'm obsessed with Ginger" or "I'm obsessed with skiing."

A practice to adopt in your quest to think well is to consider as many definitions and usages of key vocabulary words in a story or field of study as possible. By examining both your own usage and that of experts or everyday word-slingers, you paint a more nuanced picture of the topic for yourself and for those with whom you talk. You'll also be more adept at interpreting the arguments of other writers and thinkers.

ACTIVITY

One way to surface definition assumptions is to use the Fab Vocab Quick-Write Process. Here's what to do:

— Quick-Write Definitions

Each time you encounter vocabulary that is essential to the study of a specific topic, first identify how you understand the terms and then note how those same words are used by the writers or thought leaders in the field. Try it now with the fabulous vocabulary associated with critical thinking.

Here are the terms you'll define in a quick-write format:

- Fact
- Interpretation
- Evidence
- Perspective
- Opinion

- Prejudice
- Bias
- Belief
- Story
- Worldview

— Instructions

1. Turn a sheet of unlined paper horizontally so it's in landscape orientation. Fold it into eighths and then smooth it out so the fold lines remain.

2. Select eight of the terms above to explore in a quick-write. Put one term at the top of each box.

Fact	Interpretation	Evidence	Opinion
Prejudice	Bias	Belief	Worldview

3. Set your timer for two minutes per word, and quick-write your definitions for each of the terms.

4. Using a dictionary (online or the old-school book kind), look up the standard definition for each term. Note the definitions on the other side of the page, on the back of the quick-write for that term.

5. Conduct an online search, picking a specific field of study. For instance, you might try "fact + definition + critical thinking." Or perhaps you might look up "prejudice + definition + political science." Read a few different sources. Add anything new you learned to the definition side of the paper.

6. When you have all three definitions—yours, the dictionary definition, and the definition from a source that aligns with a field of study—compare them. Notice where there is consensus and where there is difference.

After you've investigated your definitions against the standard usage, you'll be able to conduct research with more clarity of purpose and understanding. You'll also be alert to any nuances the writer is bringing that you haven't seen before. You might suggest that a sibling or parent quick-write about the same terms and then compare

FACT: A fact is irreducible information that can't be disputed.

INTERPRETATION: An interpretation is what we say about the facts. It focuses on meaning, reasons, motivations, and how the facts fit into a story.

EVIDENCE: Evidence is the source material used to justify an interpretation of a fact. Think about a murder: the fact is that a gun killed a person. The interpretation is that it is a murder. The evidence is that the gun belongs to a person who hated the victim.

PERSPECTIVE: Perspective is about seeing—what you see, how you see it, why you see it the way you do, and what you don't see yet.

OPINION: A well-crafted opinion is one for which you've considered a variety of perspectives (not merely your own), examined research, and reached a conclusion (for now). An opinion is a claim you make after interpreting the data—a judgment based on facts.

PREJUDICE: Prejudice is not based on data but on faulty assumptions that often draw on stereotypes.

BIAS: A bias is when you use your own experience as the reference point for the view you adopt. Bias usually implies that you rely too heavily on your own interpretation.

BELIEF: A belief is a conviction that is shaped by religion, identity, and culture. A belief does not rely on evidence but springs from a cluster of ideas you choose for yourself.

STORY: A story is the narrative we create and tell to bring together all those intersecting pieces of data, opinion, beliefs, and perspective to explain reality as we see it. The story includes motivations, analysis, perspective, bias, and opinion—all wrapped together to make the maximum meaning from the data.

WORLDVIEW: A worldview is exactly what the compound noun says—it's how you **view** your **world**. Worldviews are more comprehensive than perspectives. A perspective is a snapshot in time. A worldview encompasses the totality of what you know and don't know. It's the lens through which you view everything—who to trust and who not to trust, what facts are important and which ones can be dismissed, which stories you believe and which ones you discredit.

your definitions. You may be surprised by the differences and even the similarities. This is super fun when you use language that is specifically generational!

Because this workbook is designed to help you think well, you ought to know how I define the terms you just explored that correspond to my book *Raising Critical Thinkers*. Keep these in mind, even if you disagree with them, as you continue to use this workbook. These are the definitions that guide the activities and their goals.

— Taking It Further

Now that you've experienced this activity with terms found in this workbook, try it again using vocabulary from a field of study that's interesting to you. It could be anything from the biological sciences to your favorite musical genre to the history of cartography (mapmaking)!

1. Identify the most important vocabulary words that go with what you are about to research. You may find them in the texts you read, in an index at the back of a book, or in a glossary on a website. Notice recurring terms. Make a list.

_____ _____

_____ _____

_____ _____

_____ _____

_____ _____

2. Fold a sheet of unlined paper in landscape orientation into eight boxes.

3. Put your terms at the top of each box. (This quick-write can accommodate up to sixteen terms, using the front and back of the page.)

4. Set the timer for two minutes per word, and one at a time, quick-write your understanding of each term until you've completed them all.

5. Look up the terms in the dictionary. Notice the contrast or similarity between definitions. Jot down some of the differences here.

_____

_____

_____

_____

_____

6. Look for definitions within the field of study where you find those terms. The researcher may provide one, or you may be able to learn more by doing an online search with the term + definition + field of study (for example, "obsessed + definition + psychology"). Notice the contrast or similarity between definitions. Jot down some of the differences here.

_____

_____

_____

_____

_____

Example

Let's say I was about to study personality disorders and ran across the word "obsessed." I would conduct a quick-write about my definition of the term: *A person who loves their hobby or favorite team or artist with a fan's pure devotion. They know a ton about the topic, and they love to share it with everyone. They spend an excessive amount of their free time thinking about and enjoying their favorites.*

Next, I would look up the term in a dictionary and then do an online search with these keywords: "obsessed + definition + psychology."

The definition I got back is: *An obsession is an unbidden, intrusive thought, image, or urge that intrudes into consciousness; attempts to dispel it are difficult and typically lead to anxiety. These thoughts, images, or urges are recognized as part of one's own mental life.*[*]

By comparing my personal definition to the clinical one, I could stay alert to how the expert's usage differs, confirms, or expands what I thought I knew at the time.

If you struggle to think of vocabulary terms, use this process to find them:

1. Free-write about the topic for seven minutes.

2. When you finish, highlight terms that strike you as pertinent to your research. For instance, if you want to examine a topic like climate change, you might notice words like "climate," "weather," and "atmosphere." You might notice these word pairs, too: "global warming," "environmental justice," or "carbon footprint." Before you research, ask yourself what these terms mean to you.

3. Use the quick-write practice (the folded paper and two-minute quick-writes) to help you identify your assumptions and personal definitions for each term. Then follow up with the dictionary and online search strategies to deepen your understanding.

4. When you begin conducting research, stay open to even more nuances.

---

* Nestadt, Paul, and Gerald Nestadt. "Obsessions." *Johns Hopkins Psychiatry Guide*, 2017. https://www.hopkinsguides.com/hopkins/view/Johns_Hopkins_Psychiatry_Guide/787020/all/Obsessions.

5. One interesting point of comparison: if you hold a definition of a term that is not accurate to the research, ask yourself where you got that erroneous definition. Is it due to a general misrepresentation in the culture? Is it because one side of the argument uses the term one way and the other side, another? Vocabulary definitions give you a clue as to the worldview or perspective of researchers and writers!

_____

_____

JOURNAL

Ask yourself the following questions:

1. Pick the most surprising definition discovery you just made. What is different about how you understand that term from how the dictionary or field of study defines it?

_____

_____

2. What new perspective did you gain?

_____

_____

3. What usages have you not heard of before?

_____

_____

4. Do you disagree with any of the definitions? If so, on what basis? Examples might include the following:

- Current usage in your age group

- Your family's usage

- What you've learned in school

- How you've read or heard this term used in the media

- How your community (religious, political, sexual identity) uses this term

_____

_____

_____

_____

_____

_____

_____

_____

_____

PART ONE: THE FOUNDATION

THE FACT STRAINER

Separating Facts from Their Fictions

(WORTH REPEATING)

BRIEF

Now that you've explored the various terms we use to think about thinking, let's get down to the facts. Facts are important for effective thinking because they're the bedrock of all arguments. A fact is *irreducible*. It's the part of the research or story that can't be altered by how we interpret it. A life skill you need, then, is to strain facts from their fictions (the stories people tell about facts). This is the part of analysis where we try to eliminate the storyteller and rely on information alone.

ACTIVITY

Let's practice identifying facts with a news item. Locate a news story you find interesting, and pick an article online that goes with it. The facts you will find in the article likely will come from these categories:

- Dates
- Names
- Verifiable activities or actions

- Locations
- Objects
- Data or research

The facts may be embedded in a story or an interpretation. Your job is to ignore the modifiers—the markers that tell you whether the name of the person means something about them; if the location is associated with a feeling, either good or bad; or if the detail is colored by adjectives meant to change how you see the data. Focus only on what is irreducible. Let's look at an example: *In New York City, a metropolis often riddled with crime, on June 15, 2023, a man, who appeared to be homeless, was found dead (murdered) next to a CVS store on 10th Avenue.*

Straining the facts from the context, you would identify these:

Facts:

- June 15, 2023
- In New York City
- A death

- A man
- Near a CVS store
- On 10th Avenue

Even the word "murdered" and the allusion to being homeless are interpretations of the facts, not facts themselves. The mention of New York City being "riddled with crime" puts you into a frame of mind that the death was necessarily a murder rather than a death not yet investigated well enough to draw that conclusion. This is how you strain facts! Your turn.

Pick a current news item and then follow these steps:

> ### *Pro tip:*
> Reading a story with a bias you don't hold sometimes makes the facts easier to strain. You can see the interpretation more easily.

1. Find multiple news sources for the story. Print several articles (three or four) if you are able.

2. Using a highlighter pen, highlight all the **FACTS** in one of the articles.

3. Go to the next article, and highlight the facts as they are stated in that article. Do the same for all the news sources.

4. Double-check to see if there are any facts omitted from any of the stories. List the facts from each story and then compare the lists. Make a note of which facts are omitted from which stories (if indeed any are). Remember, *facts are irreducible.*

_____

_____

_____

_____

_____

_____

_____

_____

_____

_____

_____

5. Notice where the facts are placed in each article—at the top, in the middle, at the bottom, or strewn throughout. You might put numbers next to the lines in the margins.

6. List the facts in the order they appear in the article in each provided space below (one per article). Read them without interpreting them.

Article 1	Article 2

Article 3	*Article 4*

JOURNAL

How does the sequence of facts impact you as a reader? What does the sequence say about the priorities of the journalist writing each article? Anything you might guess? Now that you've read multiple stories about the same topic, are any of the facts you identified interpretations, rather than facts? For instance, if you're reading about a shooting, are the motives of the shooter spoken of as fact or suggested as possible? If you're reading about a wildfire, is the cause described as a fact or a theory? Identifying facts first helps neutralize the influence of the writer's interpretation. Reading the same story multiple times makes it easier to strain the facts from the interpretation. Once you know the facts, you're free to examine the various viewpoints of the journalists. You're on your way to forming your own opinion!

ITCH TO FIT

Using Context and Discernment to Problem-Solve

(ONE TIME)

BRIEF

Have you ever noticed that if someone sings a song you know well, and they stop singing partway through, your mind supplies the rest of the lyrics? That's your brain satisfying an itch—the itch is the missing lyric. Your mind searches its catalog of song lyrics and finds the one that "fits." We call this the "itch-to-fit" pattern of learning.

Now imagine that a song you know well comes on the radio. The music is familiar, but when you pay attention, you realize the lyrics are not right. Your brain wakes up. Your curiosity is clicked on. You want to know why! You pay better attention to the lyrics. This time you discover that you're listening to a satirical version of the song. After attentive listening, you discover that this version of the familiar song is by "Weird Al" Yankovic, the musical artist who writes satires of popular songs. The mild provocation of familiar music with unfamiliar lyrics is experienced like a mosquito bite on the brain—an itch of curiosity. Your mind will now seek to "fit" this new information into a familiar, meaningful structure. Because you know the original song, your pleasure in the humorous lyrics is heightened. You'll spot the irony, the similar rhyme schemes, and the clever juxtaposition of the two different song settings. In fact, you'll even hear the old version of the song with more appreciation for its message because your mind will automatically compare it to the new version.

As it turns out, your hunger to satisfy that itch—to understand abstract information—begins as a craving for dopamine, the pleasure hormone. Curiosity comes through the same primal pathway that we associate with food cravings, falling in love, or going to a rock concert! They're all dopamine-delivery systems. One of the ways your bright brain supports your intellectual development, then, is through tapping into the itch-to-fit dopamine-drenched experience of learning. When you know just enough about a topic that your curiosity is piqued, but not so much that you're bored by the subject, your mind is quick to learn, because it makes you happy!

Here are a few examples of how you can use the itch-to-fit practice now:

- When you read a book and run across a new vocabulary word, your mind defines the unfamiliar term using the context of the surrounding paragraph. You take your cues from other words you know to help guess at the possible meaning of the word you don't know.

- If you purchase a board game that pits the players against the game itself, you'll use your familiarity with other board games that pit players against each other to help you reinterpret your competitive strategies into collaborative ones for the new game.

- When you know how to play the piano, it's easier to learn to play the guitar. Even though the finger activity for each one is completely different, you'll fit your understanding of how musical notation works to the new context for the guitar.

- Each time you level up in math, your mind is provoked into a new itch-to-fit pattern. You use your prior knowledge (addition) to help you wrap your brain around a new math process (subtraction). You use your understanding of geometry to help you grasp trigonometry.

- Because you know your native language fluently, your attention to word order is automatic and unconscious. When you learn a new-to-you language, you become aware of the importance of word order to achieve meaning and understand your own language freshly.

- When you grasp smaller distances (measurable by yardsticks), your brain can build a mental model for distances of other scales (miles, light-years).

ACTIVITY

One of the best ways to tap into your itch-to-fit experience of learning is to work with invented language and the study of grammar. In this exercise, you'll examine the famous poem "Jabberwocky" from *Through the Looking-Glass and What Alice Found There* by Lewis Carroll (the sequel to *Alice's Adventures in Wonderland*). The goal of this activity is to help you recognize two powerful factors in how our minds make meaning:

1. How the phonetic sounds of the unfamiliar term call forth similar words in our minds to give us a handhold for possible meaning-making

2. How the context surrounding an unfamiliar term provokes us to generate possible meanings

Let's start by taking a look at the two opening lines of Carroll's poem:

'Twas brillig, and the slithy toves
Did gyre and gimble in the wabe:

In the first two lines, we're confronted with brand-new vocabulary, invented by Carroll: "brillig," "slithy toves," "gyre," "gimble," "wabe." These words sound a lot like English but have no identifiable, objective definitions. Yet even without definitions, our minds give the invented words meaning.

For instance, what do you think "brillig" means? It has the "br" of "bright" and the "g" of "gloomy." Either of these meanings could make grammatical sense. After all, "'twas" is often followed by an adjective. Because that's the case, it's easy to want to supply one.

On further reflection, though, sometimes "'twas" might be followed by a noun. Couldn't "brillig" also be a season or a month of the year or a time of day, like "spring" or "January" or "afternoon"? And wouldn't those words be nouns rather than adjectives?

As you make your way through the poem, see what other meanings you might find for the invented terms, letting the sounds and familiar sentence structures guide you. To maintain a consistent storyline, you'll have to keep in mind the choices you make and how those definitions might influence your definition for the next invented term. Make a list on a sheet of paper or in a document on your computer. Test your ideas to see all the possibilities.

Your last step will be to create a lexicon with your own definitions, identifying the part of speech you assigned to the invented term that works with the context of the poem. One of the delightful by-products of this process is the realization that the same term can be understood as more than one part of speech depending on how you define it. If you want a real challenge, do this process twice, changing the meanings, and see if you can drive an entirely different interpretation, or storyline, of the poem.

Your turn!

- Do an online search for the poem "Jabberwocky" by Lewis Carroll.

- Triple space and print a copy of the poem.

- Work through the poem stanza by stanza. Highlight any word you don't know. You may highlight an English term, and that's okay! You can apply the same strategies to words in English.

- Next, notice your impression of the meaning of the words. Ask yourself why you think the words "gyre" and "gimble" call up word pairs like these: "silly" and "spirited," "reckless" and "bumbling," or "suspicious" and "careful."

- Substitute each of your English versions of the words for the invented language, and discover how those meanings impact the storyline of the poem.

- Identify what grammatical role the term plays in the stanza based on your definition, and note that, too. For instance, ask yourself what a "wabe" is. Do the "gyre" and "gimble" definitions influence how you see a wabe and its personality? Is a wabe a person, place, thing, or idea? Nouns can be any of these. How does it change the poem's meaning for wabe to be an idea like love or hate rather than an animal or monster or person or plant?

- How do the sounds of the invented words impact the definitions you give them? Do they remind you of other English words? Which ones?

After you have all the words defined and sorted, consider writing a stanza or two as a sequel using some of Carroll's invented language based on your definitions of the terms.

_____

_____

_____

_____

JOURNAL

It's wild to realize that Carroll created a meaningful poem rife with language we don't understand, yet somehow we *do* believe we've understood it. We make meaning of any words we read, and we think we understand them, too, assigning even familiar words automatic definitions without asking questions. The deep dive into "Jabberwocky" is a great starting point to discover that our subjectivity plays a role in how we read any text. Our impressions form our interpretations. Our interpretations shape our opinions and beliefs.

Answer any of these reflection questions:

- What story did you think "Jabberwocky" told before you defined the invented language?

- How did your understanding change after you defined the words for yourself? Or did it?

- Did you revise any of the initial meanings you picked after you read further into the story?

- What story do you think the poem tells now that you've worked through it word by word?

- What other possible storylines could be justified by a different interpretation of the terms?

LESSON SIX:

SILENT FILMS

Understanding the Influence of Images

(WORTH REPEATING)

BRIEF

When you read the word "cheeseburger," what reaction do you have? Pause for a moment and notice. Do you see a thick, juicy burger in a fluffy sesame seed bun, topped with melted cheese, hot from the grill, sitting on a ceramic plate at a local eatery? Do you salivate a little and wish you could eat that burger right now? Or do you imagine a dry, not quite warm, thin, gray patty on a flat white bread bun, tucked inside a fast-food wrapper? Does your mind wander to the mistreatment of animals for the food industry? Perhaps your body registers slight revulsion. You know you would never eat this burger.

This shows how the same prompt—cheeseburger—can produce wildly different interpretations of what it means to different people.

Your reactions happen instantly, triggered by the silent film your mind flashes before you. Those mental images have been created through your experiences, your research, and your personal stories. If you grew up vegetarian, you'll react to the cheeseburger with a completely different body sense than someone who grew up eating meat.

Your thinking grows when you include more perceptions than the ones that occur to you naturally. The first step is to notice and identify your reactions. The second step is to consider additional vantage points—the pictures that occur to other people. For instance, when you think about a cheeseburger, what other aspects of it have you not considered? If your immediate reaction is that it would be tasty, can you expand your thinking to consider how the meat is sourced or the nutritional impact of the fats on your body? Perhaps some people don't eat meat or may not pair meat with cheese for religious reasons. Does that expand your understanding of how a cheeseburger might be seen by others?

If your immediate response is revulsion, does that knee-jerk reaction shift if you knew that cheeseburgers ordinarily destined for the trash were being saved and provided, free of charge, to people with food insecurity? Is there a reason some people might benefit from cheeseburgers that you haven't considered?

ACTIVITY

Let's call forth your silent films around topics that are super familiar to you—images you take for granted. Make a list of immediate images that pop into your mind for each of the following items. Use the questions below this list to prompt your mind to consider both familiar, automatic images and to expand to include some possible images you hadn't considered before. Ready?

Music:

- Rock and roll
- Country
- Rap

Winter sport athletes:

- Skier
- Snowboarder
- Figure skater

Popular drinks:

- Coca-Cola
- Orange juice
- Coffee

Political actions:

- Riot
- Protest
- Rally

— Questions

Use the columns that follow to write about these prompts:

- **LIST:** Make a list of all the images you associate with each topic in each category.

- **CONSIDER:** Who do you associate with the topic (what sort of person, age, race, gender, region of the country or world), what's the setting, where does the topic happen, and how is the topic performed? Are there any exceptions you can call to mind? Jot those down.

- **ASK:** What's the difference between a rapper and a rock musician, or a skier and a snowboarder? Is there a difference between a person who prefers orange juice and someone who prefers coffee? How do you differentiate a protest from a riot? Pit the various concepts against each other to get a more nuanced view of any one of the topics.

- **REVIEW:** Are there any *other* depictions of your topic that you didn't think of right off the bat? For instance, if you picture male rock stars, what about the women in rock and roll? Do they share the same properties, or did you have to shift your silent film about what a rock and roll star might look like to accommodate them differently? Make note of those differences.

Music

Rock and roll	Country	Rap
_____	_____	_____
_____	_____	_____
_____	_____	_____
_____	_____	_____
_____	_____	_____
_____	_____	_____
_____	_____	_____
_____	_____	_____
_____	_____	_____
_____	_____	_____
_____	_____	_____
_____	_____	_____

Winter Sport Athletes

Skier	Snowboarder	Figure skater

Popular Drinks

Coca-Cola   Orange juice   Coffee

_____   _____   _____

_____   _____   _____

_____   _____   _____

_____   _____   _____

_____   _____   _____

_____   _____   _____

_____   _____   _____

_____   _____   _____

_____   _____   _____

_____   _____   _____

_____   _____   _____

_____   _____   _____

Political Actions

Riot

Protest

Rally

_____ _____ _____

_____ _____ _____

_____ _____ _____

_____ _____ _____

_____ _____ _____

_____ _____ _____

_____ _____ _____

_____ _____ _____

_____ _____ _____

_____ _____ _____

_____ _____ _____

_____ _____ _____

JOURNAL

What did you learn from the above exercise? What surprised you or confirmed what you expected?

_____

_____

_____

_____

_____

_____

_____

_____

_____

_____

_____

SILENT FILMS AND SOCIAL ISSUES

Connecting Opinions to Images

(WORTH REPEATING)

BRIEF

You've warmed up your imagination to notice particular assumptions you make about a topic the moment it hits your conscious awareness. Many of the associations were likely stereotypes, or the most commonly associated images with those items. The purpose of this next activity is to help you notice those automatic stereotypes and then to expand your thinking to include additional aspects of the topic that are less immediately apparent to you.

ACTIVITY

In this exercise, you're going to look at the ways the images in your mind shape how you think about hot-button issues. I've provided a list, but feel free to add your own. This activity can be done multiple times; simply select a new topic.

1. The first time, pick a topic that provokes a strong reaction.

2. The second time, pick a topic that doesn't evoke a strong belief or opinion.

_____

3. The third (and fourth and fifth) time: you choose!

_____

Social issues:

- **COLLEGE ATHLETES:** Should they be paid to play?

- **PHOTO EDITING AND FILTERING TOOLS:** Is it ethical to alter the faces and bodies of models in advertising or of influencers on social media?

- **AFFIRMATIVE ACTION:** Is it important for colleges to improve the chances for select students to be admitted based on race?

- **HOMESCHOOL REGULATIONS:** Should parents be allowed to teach their children without accountability to the state?

- **VIOLENT VIDEO GAMES:** Does play of such games increase aggressive and dangerous behavior?

- **GENDER-BASED TOYS:** Should toys be marketed to cater to a specific gender?

- **ANIMAL RIGHTS:** Is it ethical to use animals in medical or cosmetic testing?

- **SOCIAL MEDIA:** Do social media companies have a responsibility to regulate their impact on minors, particularly around sexuality, body dysmorphia, and bullying?

- **CELL PHONES:** Are laws restricting cell phone use while driving appropriate?

- **MUSIC AND FILMS:** Is it ethical to download music and films for free?

- **CURRICULUM:** Who has the right to decide what interpretation of history ought to be taught in kindergarten through twelfth grade?

Directions:

1. Select a topic from the list above.

2. Read the questions below, and jot down your answers. Don't worry about spelling accuracy or complete sentences. If you need to pause to close your eyes to see the image more clearly, do so! Move the camera lens of your mind around to see more detail. Not all the questions will be relevant for each topic. Skip the ones that aren't a match.

— Topic:

_____

Questions:

- When you stop to think of your topic, what scenes flash before your mind? Describe them in as much detail as possible. Then go on to the next questions to add more detail.

_____

_____

_____

_____

_____

- Do you see people? What skin tones? Can you identify gender? Consider a wide array of people, not only the ones you are used to seeing. Under-resourced, middle class, or wealthy? What sort of clothing are they wearing? Are they adults or kids? Are they from a religious group? If so, which one(s)? What foods do they enjoy? If you were to get them a hot drink, what would it be?

_____

_____

_____

_____

_____

- Where do they live? House? Apartment? Condominium? Yurt? Tent? Rural, urban, or suburban setting? What kinds of activities do they do in their homes? Are they sitting, standing, cooking, cleaning, watching television, working on a hobby, working at home, eating a meal, studying, or praying? What is the ratio of children to adults? Who's in charge? Who likes being there? Who doesn't? How do you know?

_____

_____

_____

_____

- Where is the primary activity conducted? In a lab? At a photoshoot? On a game controller? In a boardroom? At a home? Via computer or cell phone?

_____

_____

_____

_____

- Can you detect the emotional state of the people? Consider some of these possibilities: content, worried, fearful, angry, fierce, indifferent, excited, purposeful, curious, convinced . . .

_____

_____

_____

_____

- Where are these scenes? In your city? In another state or country? In your living room? Indoors or outdoors? On a set?

_____

_____

_____

- What's the weather like? What season of the year? What colors or absence of color? Warm or cold? More than one season?

_____

_____

- What do you see in the room, yard, campus, or lab? Are there new scenes crowding into the original one as you think more about your topic? What are they, and what do you make of them?

_____

_____

- If your topic were on a billboard, what would be on it?

_____

_____

- If your topic were a photo without words, what would you put in the picture?

_____

_____

- If your topic were a meme on social media, what image and message would it use?

_____

_____

- If your topic relies on equipment, what kind is it? What is the ideal equipment for this topic? Safe or unsafe? Expensive or affordable?

_____

_____

- If your topic were an ad, would it be pro or against? What images or story would show that perspective? Is there a brand that currently promotes your viewpoint with their own ads? Picture it in your head now. What brand is it?

_____

_____

_____

_____

The images you summoned in your mind influence how you read articles and books about your topic. They impact how you listen to news reports and what you feel when you meet people who make up these groups. Your silent films shape your own vocabulary you use to talk about the topic. You've named, noted, and identified those impressions. Now it's time to interpret.

JOURNAL

Reflect on what you've just learned:

- What did you discover that surprised you about the images you saw in your mind's eye?

_____

_____

- Did any of the questions trigger a change in how you see your topic? For instance, if you were to think about home education, perhaps you only ever imagined it in a house. Maybe the question about apartments made you consider that, yes, some families may homeschool in apartments.

_____

_____

- How did the original picture about the topic influence how you think about the topic?

_____

_____

- When you think about your topic now, after this inventory, name your overall impression or disposition toward the topic. Is it positive or negative? More or less familiar? Any shift from before you began? Did you find new information you hadn't considered?

_____

_____

_____

_____

_____

_____

HEADLINES AND CHYRONS

How News Media Push a Viewpoint

(WORTH REPEATING)

BRIEF

In the first few activities, you read about several key ways information is delivered: through a storyteller's viewpoint, by using vocabulary that relates to the topic, by organizing the facts in a specific sequence, and by drawing on familiar or unfamiliar images to shape how you understand the story. News organizations are masters of directing your thinking, even when you aren't aware of it! They will get you thinking in a specific direction before you've read one word of an article or listened to a single syllable of a news broadcast. Journalists use headlines, and the visual news media use what are called "chyrons" (pronounced *kie*-rons). A chyron is the text at the bottom of the television screen that tells you what the show hosts are discussing.

These two tools are meant to guide your thinking. Headlines need to grab your attention and attract you to the article that follows. Some website headlines are what we call "clickbait," designed to get you to look because they're so salacious, startling, or scandalous. Other headlines attempt neutrality: "We're just here to report the news, ma'am."

Media chyrons have three functions. First, they can alert you to breaking news, or news that breaks into regularly scheduled programming, like a shooting or a declaration of war or an earthquake. Some chyrons add detail to the news story, such as statistics or the name of a commentator. Second, they can add editorial detail that indicates what position this journalist is applying to the news. Sports channels often make use of the editorial-style chyron—wondering, for instance, if a particular athlete is "past his prime" based on a poor performance in the tournament. Third, chyrons can provide updated data in real time and even correspond to topics trending on Twitter. Remember in 2020 when the coronavirus updates were seen daily on all news channels? Election results and sports scores are often seen on scrolling chyrons.

Headlines and chyrons are powerful forces in shaping our opinions, particularly if we consistently rely on one source of information and news. One way to identify their influence is to deliberately seek additional news sources to compare the variety of ways events in the world are described by different journalists. Remember, we always want to ask, "Says who?"

ACTIVITY

Once you start to see headlines and chyrons as tools that impact how you think, you won't ever read them the same way again! In this activity, your job is to collect headlines and chyrons from a variety of news outlets. Then you'll examine how they are designed to sway your thinking in a particular direction. Whenever you find yourself baffled by why someone sees the world so differently from you, remember this activity. Most of us drink from the same fountain every day and forget that we're being slowly shaped by the most dramatic bits of news we consume.

Headlines:

1. Pick a newsworthy topic of the day. Any news event can work, but it's particularly helpful if the item has a bit of controversy built into it. Crime, elections, weather events, war, social issues, sports, and the arts are all good categories to explore.

2. When you've selected your topic, find several news outlets (four or five) that have written articles about that topic. You might look at national news (like *The New York Times* or *The Washington Post*), local news

(like your hometown television news channel's website), web-based news (like *The Daily Beast* or *National Review*), and any of the cable television news websites.

3. Without reading the articles, simply identify the headlines for the same news story in each location. Take a screenshot of each one so you capture the font size and style as well.

4. Print the screenshots of the headlines onto individual sheets of paper.

5. Lay them side by side on the floor or a table. Add a sheet of blank paper for each headline to answer the following questions:

   a. What are the facts revealed in the headline? (Revisit Part One, Lesson Four: The Fact Strainer.) Jot these down for each headline.

   b. What mood does the headline inspire? Notice adjectives in particular. Check all that apply:

☐ Confidence	☐ Hopelessness
☐ Fear	☐ Vindication
☐ Worry	☐ Suspicion
☐ Triumph	☐ Trust
☐ Anger/outrage	

   c. Does the headline make you want to read more? Why?

   d. Notice the differences in emphasis among headlines. For instance, in which headlines are details more important than people? Notice the source for these. Are people described with adjectives? Which ones? Can you tell if you are supposed to think well or poorly of anyone from the headline? What was your clue?

   e. Now read a couple of the articles. How similar or dissimilar are they? Do the headlines match the content? Does what you read at the top match the tone of the article?

f. Now that you've examined the news item by reading about it, what headline would you write? Write one headline that pushes a particular viewpoint. Then write one that tries to be as objective and neutral as possible. Finally, write a headline that is pure clickbait!

_____

_____

_____

Chyrons:

1. Grab a notebook or clipboard and paper for this activity.

2. Pick a cable news or sports channel. Watch the chyrons for thirty minutes.

3. Jot down the various chyrons you see. If you need to pause the television show to jot them down correctly, do it! If you prefer to take photos with your phone, that works, too.

4. Sort the chyrons you saw into these three categories:

    a. Breaking news

    b. Editorial content

    c. Up-to-date information (like sports scores or election results)

5. Ask yourself: Is the information in the "breaking news" chyron actually breaking? Or are they merely using that tag to grab your attention? What constitutes breaking news?

6. Is the editorial content clear, or does the chyron give the appearance of essential fact? (This will be a judgment call on your part.) Notice any language meant to provoke an emotional reaction like outrage or "gotcha!"

7. How useful is the scrolling information? How frequently does it change?

8. If you have time, flip to another channel in the same genre (news, sports). Notice what is similar and what is different. Especially notice if the same topic is addressed using different language. Why do you think that is? What is the different goal of this channel?

9. Write three of your own chyrons for the topics you saw in your thirty minutes: one that focuses on breaking news, one that reveals an opinion you hold, and one that includes up-to-date information.

_____

_____

_____

JOURNAL

Now that you've reviewed headlines and chyrons, journal your reflections. What did you learn about the way these blasts of information influence how you think? Who did you trust and why? Who did you distrust and why? Is there a new source of information you might want to read or watch that you hadn't before? Why? The way information is introduced sets a tone for how it is received. Our text messages, social media updates, and email subject lines are all versions of chyrons and headlines if you think about it. They are bite-sized bits of information we hope will influence how the reader thinks about what follows!

_____

_____

_____

SPOT THE MISINFORMATION!

Vetting Statistics and Data

(WORTH REPEATING)

BRIEF

Have you ever believed a lie? I have. I used to believe that the Great Wall of China was visible from space. Truth is, it's not visible by the naked eye from space and certainly not from the moon. The only chance to see the wall from space is at low Earth orbit with magnification, and only then under perfect visibility conditions. The rumor that the Great Wall is the only man-made structure visible from space was started in 1938, and Chinese national pride fed it. When Chinese astronaut Yang Liwei went to space in 2003, to everyone's shock, he reported that he could not see the Great Wall from space. He overturned a "fact" everybody thought they knew. This revelation plunged the Chinese education system into a tizzy. Their textbooks had been boldly making the claim of the Great Wall's visibility from space for decades.

Just because a belief has been widely accepted as true doesn't mean it's a fact. Because I cared to know the truth about the Great Wall's visibility from space, I conducted research. I used tools to help me evaluate the claims and the evidence. In the end, I concluded that my belief was in error. To be a critical thinker, it takes curiosity and courage to examine an automatically accepted "fact" and then to overturn a belief you've taken for granted.

The most essential tool in the critical thinking toolkit is *caring*. A quality thinker has to care enough to double-check "facts," to identify credible sources, and to offer reasonable interpretations of events or actions. It means knowing that just because someone provides a link on social media, that's not proof the information is accurate. Caring to think well depends on two essential practices that anyone can learn. In this next activity, you'll ask yourself these two questions each time you encounter important information:

- How is this information measured?

- What are its benchmarks?

How information is measured helps you identify the way information is packaged.

- Is an item measured by size, color, weight, shape, speed, distance, frequency, or volume?

- Is a historical event measured by era, reign of a particular leader, size of an empire, outcome of a conflict, or effect on a population?

- Is a world record measured by speed, force, duration, weight, distance, temperature, length, or count?

When you know what sort of record you are evaluating, you'll want to know which measurement tool was used—speed measured in miles or kilometers per hour, temperature measured in Fahrenheit or Celsius, ratio of attempts to successful outcomes or absolute numbers, conquests of populations or land acquisitions, counting by activity or the resulting points scored? Consider this example: in absolute baskets, one basketball player may have scored more baskets but accumulated fewer points than another ball player if those baskets were mostly two-pointers rather than three-pointers. Number of baskets successfully made is a different statistic from the number of points scored. How information is measured is critical to understanding the facts being asserted!

Benchmarks, on the other hand, are those statistics in a field of study that establish its norms. For instance, if you hear a weather report for a place you've never been, you may not be able to determine if the weather is typical or exceptional. To learn which it is, you'd begin by making sure you knew if the unit of measurement was Fahrenheit or Celsius. (Twenty degrees Fahrenheit and twenty degrees Celsius are entirely different forecasts!) Then you'd identify the average temperature in that unit of measure for that time of year in that place. Finally, you'd compare the current forecast against the benchmark. So if someone told you it was twenty degrees in January in Corpus Christi, Texas, what would your first question be? You'd want to know: Is that temperature in Fahrenheit or Celsius? Twenty degrees Fahrenheit is below freezing, whereas twenty degrees Celsius is warm and pleasant. As it turns out, Corpus Christi is typically warm and pleasant in January—twenty degrees Celsius is the average temperature. Twenty degrees Fahrenheit would be shockingly cold.

Let's look at another example in sports. If someone tells you that a runner ran a marathon in sixty minutes, would you know if that was a realistic statistic? If you're a runner, you may know right away. But what if you aren't? The only way you could validate or dispute that assertion is if you knew how runners measure their performance in racing (minutes per mile) and the established benchmarks of pace for elite runners.

First, you'd make a note of the distance of a standard marathon (26.2 miles). Then you'd want to find out how quickly an elite distance runner runs a mile. The benchmark for superfast distance runners is about 4 to 5 minutes per mile. If you multiply 4 minutes by 26.2 miles, the runner would need at least 104 minutes (44 more minutes than an hour) to complete the race. Therefore, the 60-minute marathon assertion fails. Without knowing the distance of the race or how fast distance runners can run a mile, it would be easy to hear that impressive statistic and pass along that misinformation! In fact, that's how it happens.

Understanding units of measure and the benchmarks of the specific field gives you the best shot at affirming truths and spotting lies. Let's test your skills.

ACTIVITY

Spot the misinformation!

Vet the following list of "facts" for accuracy. Your job is to ask two questions of each item: "How is it measured?" and "What are its benchmarks?" Then, draw a conclusion. See if you can identify the misinformation and then correct it!

- The population of Calgary, in Alberta, Canada, is experiencing explosive growth.

  - **ASK**: What is the current population of Calgary? What are the boundaries of Calgary? Does that include suburbs or just the city proper? What is the ordinary growth of that population, or the average growth for a decade year over year? What is this year's growth? What does the word "explosive" mean related to population growth?

- Tennis star Naomi Osaka hit the fastest serve ever for a woman at 195 miles per hour.

  - **ASK**: What is the fastest tennis serve by a woman? How was it measured—miles per hour or kilometers per hour? Does this statistic align with that finding?

- The tallest mountain in the world is Mt. Everest.

  - **ASK**: How are mountains measured—from sea level or taking into account landmass underwater? What is the tallest mountain for each of these measuring standards? What measurement method is the preferred method among geologists?

In this quick examination of three types of measurements, you can see that it matters to ask questions of statistics before assuming that a report made into a pretty graphic online or onscreen is automatically correct.

JOURNAL

Each of us has overturned a belief at some point in our lives. For instance, you might have started your young life believing that the moon followed your car when you drove at night. Perhaps you believed that the music you heard on the radio was performed by real band members playing their music inside a radio station (not prerecorded music broadcast through a machine). What caused you to change your belief? Chat with a parent or sibling to help you remember a belief you held that you have since overturned, if you have difficulty remembering one. Then, think about how you challenged your belief as you gained more information. What finally convinced you to leave that belief behind?

_____

_____

_____

_____

_____

_____

_____

_____

_____

_____

PART ONE: THE FOUNDATION

RED FLAGS WAVING

Examining a Source for Its Credibility

(WORTH REPEATING)

BRIEF

When studying a topic, you'll run into a glut of information online. One way to ensure you're barking up the right tree of research is to look for red flags. In a dating relationship or friendship, we use "red flags" to help us determine whether or not the other person is a good match. Is the person you're dating controlling? Are they expecting an exclusive commitment too quickly? Does that person make fun of you, or express hostility or jealousy? Do they lie? Just because you like someone doesn't mean they're good for you.

The same thing goes for research. Just because the information feels right or is presented in a professional-looking way on a website doesn't mean it's reliable or accurate. Information online, or anywhere, really, is presented with an agenda—to get you to accept the information! Some websites give the impression of objectivity while others openly rant an opinion. Neither posture, by the way, guarantees accuracy. Neither guarantees inaccuracy either.

My suggestion? Look at any information you consume online or in a book or on social media as a "dating profile." That "profile" is designed to hook you—to get you to fall for the interpretation of the information being offered. In order to avoid being manipulated into poor judgment, you need a set of questions you can ask to identify the red flags of poorly researched and unreliable information. That way, you can say, "Nope! Not a match for reliability or facts!" and move on.

ACTIVITY

The acronym CACAO is a great place to start when doing research. Here's what it stands for:

- **C**urrency: Is the information up to date?

- **A**ccuracy: Is this information corroborated or confirmed in other sources?

- **C**overage: Is enough detail provided? Are there citations to support?

- **A**uthority: Are the author's credentials easy to find and valid? Is the organization reputable?

- **O**bjectivity: Does the source acknowledge multiple possible interpretations or competing claims?

In this activity, the objective is to conduct online research using the CACAO rubric. I've translated the above questions into "red flags" to help you do this research.

Red flags:

1. **CURRENCY:** How old is this information? How frequently is this kind of data measured? (For instance: a population census occurs every ten years in the United States, so if the data in the report you are reading is from twenty years ago, it's too old to consider for a current event.)

2. **ACCURACY:** How is the information collected (firsthand experience, in a lab, by experts, at a competition)? How do I know this information is true? Who else agrees? Who disagrees? Is it a commonly held belief or a factual conclusion?

3. **COVERAGE:** What's missing from this representation of the information? Who else has a stake in this discussion? Are they mentioned here?

4. **AUTHORITY:** Who does this "information collector and presenter" think they are? On what basis does this person or organization have the right to express this information? What are their credentials? Do I find their credentials credible? Why or why not? Who is challenging their authority? Do they have a valid challenge to offer?

5. **OBJECTIVITY:** What is the presenter trying to get me to believe? How much room do they give to counterclaims? Do I feel pushed to adopt their position? Would the opposition recognize themselves in the description of their position by this thinker?

Using the questions above, select a controversial issue. A hint for finding an issue: put any topic plus the word "controversy" in an online search engine, and you will land square in the middle of a hotly debated topic. You might put "TikTok + controversy" into a search engine, for example, and discover that there are national security issues related to the app that are hotly debated in the United States.

Once you've identified a topic that is controversial, click through to an article about that topic. Now, walk through the red flags questions and fill in your comments. Don't worry too much about whether or not you've done this exercise "right." The goal is to train your mind to ask these questions whenever you read any information. The place to begin is in the asking. Over time, your skill at spotting disinformation and unreliable sources will grow.

Topic + article title:

_____

1. **CURRENCY:** How old is the information?

_____

2. **ACCURACY:** How do I know this information is true?

_____

3. **COVERAGE:** What's missing from this article?

_____

_____

4. **AUTHORITY:** Who does the presenter think they are?

_____

5. **OBJECTIVITY:** What is the presenter trying to get me to believe?

_____

_____

_____

_____

You may not be able to answer each question in depth, but it's important to at least ask the question. By developing this habit of mind, you are less likely to be swept up in emotion or someone else's agenda. Apply these questions to any link a friend sends you, any textbook chapter assigned by a teacher, and any research you do when writing a paper. Walking through these questions is the first step in doing quality research. You'll discover quickly who makes a good match!

By the way, we're entering a period of information dissemination that is more fraught with error and disinformation than ever. With the advent of artificial intelligence and deepfakes, it's especially easy to be misled. Remember, just because ChatGPT or a TikTok video using someone's actual voice passes before your eyes and ears doesn't mean you're getting factual, evidence-based information.

JOURNAL

What did you learn from this search? Did you discover any missing information or bias? Did your own understanding deepen, or did you feel that what you know was never meaningfully addressed in the article? What other questions occurred to you as you read? Take a few moments to journal about your experience.

_____

_____

_____

_____

_____

_____

_____

_____

_____

_____

_____

_____

PART ONE: THE FOUNDATION

IDENTITY AND THE WORLDVIEW GRID

How Personal Perceptions and Community Values Shape Us

(ONE TIME)

BRIEF

You're a person who has formed a solid, reliable identity. This identity influences you all day, every day, even when you aren't paying attention to it. Your identity comes from an intersection of the ways you learn about the world and your place in it. Because we sometimes take our identities for granted, it can be difficult to notice when they influence how we interpret or perceive what we are told or taught.

One way to identify the features of your identity is to ask yourself a set of self-examination questions each time you consider information. For instance, take one of the following topics and name what you believe about it. Then, ask the following questions and write your answers in the space provided.

Topics for the next two activities:

- **A WOMAN CHANGING HER SURNAME WHEN SHE GETS MARRIED:** Is it necessary, optional, or shouldn't happen?

- **HUNTING FOR SPORT:** Is it ethical or not?

- **VIOLENT VIDEO GAMES:** Does playing them create violent people, or are the games benign sources of entertainment?

- **DATING:** What's the right age to date, if ever, and why?

- **US ELECTORAL SYSTEM:** Should elections be determined by the electoral college or popular vote?

Questions:

- Where do I get my perspective?

_____

_____

- Why do I think that?

_____

- What source provided the information I have?

_____

- Why do I accept the authority of the source of this information?

_____

_____

- How do I know I'm right?

_____

_____

- What other perspectives have I heard or considered?

  _____

  _____

- What's at stake in my belief? What would it cost me to change my opinion?

  _____

  _____

- What do I think _____ [name an authority, friend, parent, religious leader, or opponent] might say about it?

  _____

  _____

- Is this what I believe, or is it what I think I should believe?

  _____

  _____

Now that you've taken your pulse on a controversial belief, let's look at the worldview grid.

LENSES	1 Individual	3 Community
FILTERS	2 Perception	4 Reason

— Lenses

Lenses are the prisms through which we look out at the world:

- As an individual (inside my skin, on my behalf)

- In a community (shared with "my people," shaped by our collective values)

— Filters

Filters adjust the lenses:

- Via perception (the way my body, emotions, and mind make meaning)

- Using reason (how my community interprets facts and figures into a story of logic I accept)

We process information as it comes to us through two primary lenses at the top of the grid: as individuals and as members of a prized community. Then we find a way to express and explain (or justify) how we interpret the world using a blend of the two filters at the bottom of the grid: perception and reason.

As an individual, you came into the world meeting your own needs. When you felt hungry (a perception of hunger), you cried to be fed. When you were tired, you slept—no matter where you were! Your individual perceptions governed how you interacted with the world.

As a member of a family—your first community—you learned habits and values from your parents, who helped you interpret your perceptions. For instance, by the time you turned two, you learned that sleeping ought to happen in a bed and that food is eaten at mealtimes and designated snack times. You modified your perceptions to match the family values, and you accepted your parents' reasoning— convenience, order, and good manners.

When it comes to why you believe what you do, you blend your personal perceptions (video games are fun!) with the logic story your family or school gives you to help you interpret that perception (video games can also become monopolizing of your time and cause you not to care about your schoolwork). This is the community story about video games that you may or may not adopt for yourself.

Pick another topic from the list on pages 73–74, and answer these questions:

Topic:

_____

1. As an individual, how do I see this topic? What would I like to be true? Why?

_____

2. When I consider my community (family, school, faith community), what story does it tell about this topic?

_____

3. Do I find the interpretation my community gives me compelling and easy to follow?

_____

4. Do I disagree and feel comfortable holding a different perspective? Why or why not?

_____

JOURNAL

There are no right or wrong answers here. Communities have a vested interest in taming human behavior and influencing groups of people to follow a set of guidelines. (Some groups even adopt a "don't follow any rules" rule!) Our job is to pay attention to how frequently our perceptions are aligned or not with the community logic story and to notice what information we need for a better-informed opinion.

We also want to pay attention to how the community regards dissent. As you reflect on the position you currently hold, what has been more valuable to you, your personal perception (experience), or your community's reasoning (logic story)? Take a moment to reflect on why you prefer one over the other. Consider experiences that you use to trump the guidance of a community you value. For instance, perhaps you've been taught that sleeping in is a sign of laziness. But you know that for you personally, sleeping extra hours on the weekend gives you the energy you need to lead a productive life.

Now consider if there are some perceptions you have personally that you gladly give up for values of your community. A small example: you love listening to loud music on big speakers but choose to use headphones for the sake of everyone's comfort in your home. A larger example: you enjoy driving fast, but you have adopted the city's speed limits because they ensure the safety of all.

_____

_____

_____

_____

_____

_____

_____

_____

_____

LESSON TWELVE:

"I AM FROM" POEM

Writing a Mini-Memoir

(ONCE A YEAR)

BRIEF

So far, you've explored a variety of ways to know more about yourself and where you come from. The next activity is so enjoyable! The time-honored "I Am From" poem is a process of noticing all the factors that add up to you. (The original poem that inspired a movement of poetry in this vein was written by George Ella Lyon: "Where I'm From.") Naturally, geographical location is part of what it means to be "from" somewhere. But we also are from a kind of cooking, from a religious or nonreligious tradition, from sounds and sights, from memories and holidays, from pain and joy. My son Liam wrote a powerful "I Am From" poem that I'd like to share here with you as an example.

Liam Bogart (fifteen years of age):

I am from the burning of Christmas trees
I am from the journaling of swirling listless leaves
I am from homemade paper cranes, haikus, and calendars
I am from Easter, pipe smoking, and golden eggs
I am from candles, lopsided beeswax
I am from nonexistent Santa myths

I am from vegan cinnamon rolls
I am from Blessing, Mr. Darcy, and the blessings of Mr. Darcy
I am from Frodo Baggins
I am from Redwall
I am from Harry Potter, *passed around in Italy*
I am from The Odyssey, *read aloud to silent children*
I am from History of the World *and a sleeping mom*
I am from The Name of the Wind *in Chicago*
I am from myopic Jake and Noah the Duke
I am from silver-tongued Caitrin and Johannah the only 6 of 5
I am from obscenities yelled over StarCraft *lost*
I am from subconsciously learned grammar, Chomsky, and Julie
I am from brave thinking and brave writing
I am from nonexistent science and Ing Wan's math
I am from homeschool, unschool, high school, and college

ACTIVITY

Ask yourself the following questions to stir up concepts to include in your own "I Am From" poem (take notes to capture your answers):

- Identify your background—ethnic, religious, cultural, nationality . . . whatever defines you for you.

- Name where you live and have lived. Describe those places with a few words, nouns or adjectives.

- Name places you've visited.

- Name your favorite foods.

- Select four adjectives to describe yourself.

- Select a few adjectives to describe your family.

- What family holidays and traditions are important to you? Think about particular traditions, too. In our family, we burn the Christmas tree in July and smoke corncob pipes on Easter.

- Name the communities you are a part of.

- What habits are your own? What habits have you learned from your community?

- What stories, songs, or legends and myths do you love?

- List two or three memorable experiences in your life. Could be a happy memory, like winning a tournament, or an unhappy one, like going in for surgery. Could be how you found a book on a tram in Chicago and read it there (like *The Name of the Wind* by Patrick Rothfuss, in Liam's poem).

- Name something sad or difficult from your memory.

- What textures, scents, tastes, and sounds do you associate with your childhood so far? Might be vanilla-scented candles or dust, or could be Lysol or chili in a slow cooker . . .

Consider these categories, too:

- Who I say I am

- Who others say I am

- Who I aspire to be

Instructions to construct your poem:

1. Take these lists and add "I am from" to the start of each phrase or word.

2. Type the list and triple space. Then print.

3. Snip the sentences into strips and rearrange them into the most pleasing sequence.

4. Staple each one to a page in the order you approve, rearrange the list on the computer, and print the final copy.

5. Feel free to embellish or change words as you read and reread. It helps to read the sentences aloud, to hear the words and sequence as you revise.

Some students prefer to handwrite the final version and illustrate it with sketches. You can write your poem in the space provided.

Identity is the foundation for all of what you do as a critical thinker. Because you're always growing and changing, you can even write a new "I Am From" poem each year and keep the poems handy as useful portraits to return to.

JOURNAL

What new aspects of yourself did you uncover through this poem-writing activity? Any surprises? Take a few minutes to reflect on the experience.

_____

_____

_____

_____

_____

_____

_____

_____

_____

_____

_____

Part Two

THE PRACTICE: GROWING YOUR THINKING SKILLS

SYMBOLIC DICTIONARY

Reading and Deciphering Symbols

(WORTH REPEATING)

BRIEF

One of the ways you grow your brilliant brain is through reading. Let me tell you what you already know: You read *constantly*. You read books, sure, and websites. But you also read text messages and online chats on Twitch. You read discussion boards and the instructions on your digital device to load a new streaming service. You read billboards and neon signs. You read captions while watching movies, TikToks, Instagram Reels, and YouTube videos.

Reading is one of the primary ways we know what we know! In addition to reading words, you read symbols with a skill your parents and grandparents envy. From emojis when texting to the symbols on your gaming devices to the graphics on your role-playing game cards, you are expert decoders. Everywhere you look, you're invited to understand a message, whether a facial expression, a stick figure, an animated GIF, the statistics of a baseball game, or a current meme on social media. It takes skillful critical thinking to decipher (decode) symbols and images.

While flying internationally, I discovered that pictographs on planes and in airports are often used to convey information to a wide variety of language speakers. Where to find restrooms and how to use a toilet, how to get to a flight's gate, which places are for food and which are for hot drinks—this information is conveyed through symbols that can guide anyone, regardless of what language or orthography system they know.

Symbols are powerful tools that require critical thinking to create and interpret! Color, size, how realistic they appear, what design indicates the action—all that careful thought goes into symbolic language and sign design. Think about how the military uses flags and Morse code. Consider how traffic is organized. Imagine the pictorial directions for building Lego kits and Ikea bookcases!

ACTIVITY

Build your own symbol system for an area of interest. You might choose hiking or card playing or computer programming or riding horses or making YouTube videos. Any interest will do—even baking muffins! Your task is to analyze the particular requirements of the activity and then build a library of symbols that would guide a novice to expert practice—all with no words. Consider the following concepts:

1. What are the steps you take to participate in this activity?

   _____

   _____

   _____

2. What equipment is needed? How is it used? What directions would someone need to use it well and appropriately?

   _____

   _____

   _____

3. Would the action be better represented by an abstract design, like a triangle or an arrow or a squiggle you create? Or should you depict the

activity with an illustration? (Likely, you'll need both.) Use the following space to draw these symbols and/or illustrations.

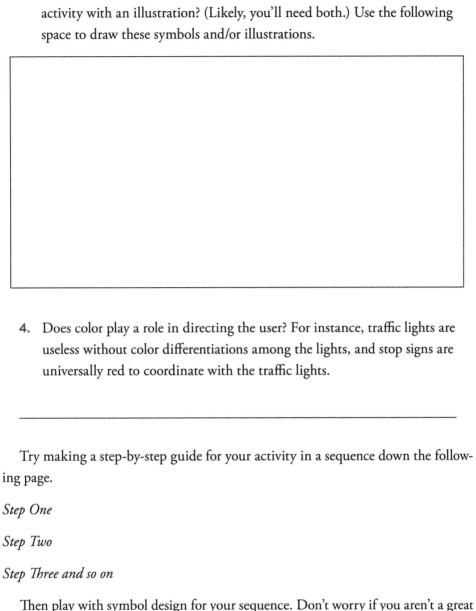

4. Does color play a role in directing the user? For instance, traffic lights are useless without color differentiations among the lights, and stop signs are universally red to coordinate with the traffic lights.

Try making a step-by-step guide for your activity in a sequence down the following page.

Step One

Step Two

Step Three and so on

Then play with symbol design for your sequence. Don't worry if you aren't a great illustrator. Go online to see if the symbols you want to use exist already (a purple square, a spray of confetti, an oval outline, a two-dimensional desktop, etc.). Print the images, cut them out, and glue them to the page. The true test of your symbolic library will be using it to guide someone else through a practice you design for them. By the way, when you create new symbols for an action, sometimes it's necessary to include a key that translates them into words or measurement sizes. Think of a legend on a map or a conversion chart on a recipe.

JOURNAL

Notice the way your mind sorts through images and symbols to create the flow you deem necessary to engage in your selected activity. Which symbols did you try and discard? Why? Which symbols feel like an excellent fit? Why? How did you select colors, if you did? What about that color matches the goal you had in mind for that step? Did you ask someone to follow the guidance from your symbols for the activity? How did that go? Did you change any of the symbols and replace them? Which ones, and why? Through this activity, what did you learn about other symbolic systems you use every day? Creating a symbolic library helps us recognize invisible assumptions, such as how a game system is played or why we think a certain step is necessary in a sequence. Each time we analyze a process or an action in terms of how someone else might follow the same steps, we shift to imagining someone else's experience. We learn how to communicate with them so they understand us better. That's the crux of critical thinking—expanding to include more experiences and perceptions when we analyze any topic under the sun!

VISUAL JOURNAL

Adding Images to Research

(WORTH REPEATING)

BRIEF

Imagine you want to take a trip somewhere you've never been. You do research—all of it in words. You read blogs or websites that have long articles but no pictures. You pick a place hoping that what you read matches the images you formed in your mind. This is how some of us traveled in the 1900s. We relied on our imaginations to guide us after reading rich descriptions in words.

Now imagine researching that same trip in the twenty-first century. You get to use websites and YouTube to see pictures and video footage of your potential destination. You scroll through hotels or Airbnb rentals, looking for the ones that inspire you. You supply your imagination with images, not just words.

Which of these two strategies do you feel gives you the best chance of having a wonderful trip? For most of us, we prefer to see an image when we research travel. We want to see that what we hope to be true in our minds is verified by the fact of what is shown to us. Naturally, there are times when the image sets us up for failure, too, when what is photographed doesn't identically match the reality upon arrival. Images can cut both ways. They can give us a greater sense of clarity about a topic, but they also can obscure, cover up, or intensify what we feel about a place.

In this activity, you're going to collect images as part of your research into a topic. Many times, when we focus exclusively on our thoughts in words, we minimize the impact of the reality of that era, topic, or experience. For instance, in the United States, one of the reasons the Vietnam War was so hotly debated is that for the first time in history, Americans watched war footage in real time on television each night. They weren't merely reading in a newspaper about a conflict in a distant land. Rather, they were eyewitnesses to the destructive power of bombs, napalm, and our young soldiers being killed on the other side of the world. It was, in a word, horrifying.

Visual imagery isn't always perfectly accurate. We know this because of both the power of photography to highlight some features and hide others and the manipulation available via photo editing. Sometimes pictures supply the needed reality check, requiring us to care. At other times, visual imagery can be used to exploit us into an unjustified mood—anger, hope, romance, or grief. The main role imagery should play is to add detail and layers to what might otherwise be mere words on a screen or page.

ACTIVITY

Take your mind on vacation! Just like in the case of real travel, you'll be noticing the images your mind creates and then comparing those to the images you find through research. Expect a little brain workout but with a fascinating landscape to enjoy in your mind's eye.

1. Select a place you've never been. You might grab a globe and play roulette, spinning it with your eyes closed until your finger lands on a country you've never visited. You might conduct an online search for the ancient wonders of the world or the UNESCO World Heritage Sites. You might look up a list of remarkable wildernesses in the world. Select a country, historic site, or wilderness for this activity.

2. Free-write for two minutes about the immediate impressions that formed in your mind when you selected the location. Even if you have never been there, your mind, which loves to make meaning, is already forming associations (beach—warm, good; arctic tundra—cold, bad). Get those all down.

3. Next, search online for images that go with your location. You can even watch some videos, if you'd like. Consider turning off the sound to get a visual experience without music or narration.

4. Collect numerous images and print them. Arrange the photos in a collage on a bulletin board, or glue them to a poster board.

5. Free-write again. Write your impressions of this site now that you've looked at images. What are the differences between what you initially thought about the site and what you know now from pictures and videos?

6. Find one or two articles to read about the location. Do the articles support the visuals? Are there key differences you missed?

This same practice can be applied to a topic you might research for a paper. For instance, any historical event of the last 150 years will have all kinds of photographic records to support your research. Keeping a bulletin board nearby for photos you can print and pin up will help you as you read more about that particular era. When studying the history of the United States in the 1900s, for instance, whether you examine the roaring 1920s or the migrant farm workers struggle of the 1950s or the civil rights movement of the 1960s, photographs and film will add depth and perspective to your research.

JOURNAL

Let's not journal with words for this activity. Instead, now that you are nearly half-way through this workbook, use the following blank page to doodle or glue images that relate to critical thinking. It may take a little cognitive flexibility, but you might find a meme online, you might pick images related to the brain, or you might want to select pictures that are a metaphor for how you feel about your progress so far (like a medal or trophy).

READING WIDELY

Curating a "Library of Variety"

(WORTH REPEATING)

BRIEF

Reading is the safest way to learn anything. You can pick up a book to read and then put it down when you get bored or annoyed. You can skip paragraphs, statistics, or information you find problematic to your opinion. Reading gives you a glimpse of a subject, but it can never give you complete information. For instance, if all your information about violins came from reading and you never actually listened to a violin being played, could you say that you *knew* the violin fully? Imagine reading about bears or lightning or the color purple without ever seeing and hearing a grizzly, witnessing a lightning strike, or noticing the rich hue of violet in a rainbow or crocus. Reading is powerful, but it's incomplete. Reading gives you information that is under your control. You get to decide whether or not you agree with it and whether to consider it important or insignificant. Reading offers details you might not directly experience, yet it lacks the capacity to give you access to the topic through your five senses.

In order to avoid the trap of reading only material that aligns with your worldview and beliefs, it's important to curate what I call a "library of variety." When you read an opinion piece, for instance, it's a good idea to look for another article that expresses a contrasting opinion on the same topic. The discipline of caring about how a topic is presented from inside each viewpoint is one way to offset the danger of reading—namely, reinforcing your own views without considering challenges.

Reading authors from a range of perspectives, backgrounds, and geographical locations is also a powerful way to expand how well you think. It's tempting to seek out writers who share your identity characteristics. Looking at the same topic through the experience and identity of someone quite different from you allows you to see through their eyes the impacts of the same issues for their particular community.

In addition to reading a wide variety of authors, it's important to read more than one kind of writing genre (or writing style). For instance, you might read a newspaper article about a devastating fire. It would also be important to read personal accounts of those impacted by the fire—home and business owners—as well as those who participate in evaluating and fighting the fire—firefighters, wilderness experts, police, scientists, and political figures. It might help to read articles that describe the process of collecting data for determining the cause of the fire, and opinion pieces that contend for more than one theory about how it started and what it would take to put it out. The more viewpoints and aspects of the fire you consider, the better you'll be able to think about the fire. Too often, we lean heavily on one source for our information, such as news headlines, opinion pieces, graphs and data, Twitter threads, or social media posts. This habit tends to skew information in a single direction. To think well, consider reading a variety of styles of writing related to the topic.

ACTIVITY

Build a library of variety!

Take an inventory of your current library. Check the box after you've taken the inventory.

☐ When I look at our bookshelves, what world do I see reflected in our book choices?

_____

☐ Which books reflect my experiences?

_____

☐ Which books help me know and learn about experiences different from mine?

_____

☐ Have we included books that explore music, science, history, geography, food, math, and art?

_____

☐ Do we have books based on research as well as those written with firsthand experience?
- **NOTE**: Neither firsthand experience nor researched-based writing automatically qualifies or disqualifies a book. It's important to read reviews from members of the community. How was the book received by those represented in this story? Is it accurate in portraying the community and/or time period? Are there some people in this group who hold a different perspective than the majority?

- Are there alternative books available that better represent the community/event/time period?

_____

_____

_____

☐ Is there a mix of authors in terms of gender, nationality, race, ability, socioeconomic status, political affiliation, and so on?

_____

☐ Is there a mix of protagonists in terms of gender, nationality, race, ability, socioeconomic status, political affiliation, and so on?

_____

☐ Is there a mix of perspectives—historical, personal, statistical, editorial, artistic, and factual?

_____

JOURNAL

What did you learn as you looked through the books available to you in your home? What new books do you need to add to your reading diet to round out your library of variety? What new online sources can you include in your reading diet? Use the space below to make a list of books you might like to find on your next trip to the library. Additionally, make a list of websites that you can add to your reading life.

_____

_____

_____

_____

_____

_____

_____

READING DEEPLY

Building Stamina for Deep Focused Attention

(WORTH REPEATING)

BRIEF

You and your brain have a problem. Back at the dawn of time, our brains were on high alert. They awaited the grunt of a warthog or a sudden downtick in temperature to alert us that it was time to act quickly. This style of attention is called "hyperfocus attention state" and is necessary for survival when your environment is risky. As human beings developed civilizations that allowed everyone to take a collective breath, we learned a new skill called "deep-focus attention state." The rise of private reading in places like monasteries, libraries, and universities gave human beings the chance to sit quietly and take in information without the distraction of fear that an ambush was about to occur.

Since the dawn of the printing press, human beings have been enrolled in a project of developing that deep-focus attention state, and it has produced massive advantages! Take a quick glance around the room you're in—the computer, the chair, the electricity running the lights, your cellphone, even the clothes you're wearing and the snack you're eating are the result of dedicated deep-focus attention to create the systems that make all those wonderful tools for living available to you.

Today, for the first time in centuries, we're sliding back into the hyperfocus attention state with a vengeance. Our technology companies are exploiting that old programming by creating algorithms designed to tap into the part of our brains that keep us on high alert. The consequence of being jarred out of reverie or reading when you hear a ping from your phone or computer is that you eject your brain from the deep-focus attention state that enables you to grow your mind and capacity for quality thinking. Add in hearts and likes and comment sections, and you can see how the hyper brain is in reaction mode at all times. One funny side effect is that we actually feel *compelled* to offer opinions on all sorts of topics before we've even had time to consider the countless variables adjacent to the idea!

The good news is that you can rewire or retrain your brain to be the deep thinker it needs to be in order to grow a wise, insightful mind.

ACTIVITY

Develop your deep-focus attention state through a reading training program!

1. Pick a book to read. Make it one you currently find challenging to stick with. And choose a print copy rather than an ebook on a digital device.

2. Dedicate a time of day to reading that book only. Follow these instructions:

    a. Put your cell phone in another room, out of sight (similar to how you'd put a bag of potato chips in the cupboard rather than leave it out on the counter if you don't want to be tempted to eat the entire bag).

    b. Set a timer for a predetermined length of time. Start with ten minutes on the first day. Build to thirty minutes of reading deeply without interruption. You can increase the amount you read each day by a minute or two.

    c. Sink into a comfortable chair or nook of the sectional. If you find it too distracting to be in the family room, consider practicing at a library or alone in your bedroom. Be sure you have good lighting. Grab your book.

    d. *Read.* That's it. When your mind is drawn away, gently redirect it to the page: "I know you want to think about X. Right now, we're reading."

e. When the timer dings, stop. Bookmark the page for the next day. Let your mind mull over what you read without drawing any specific conclusions.

Continue this practice until you can feel how your brain shifts and quiets once you sit long enough and give attention to what you're reading.

JOURNAL

Here are five journal prompts. Use one each day this week that you sink into your deep reading habit.

— Day One

Pick a word that jumped out at you while you read. It could be a theme, like "injustice" or a quirky term, like "cornucopia." You might pick the name of a character (if you're reading fiction) or a historical figure (if you're reading nonfiction). Write the word or name at the top of your writing space and then free-write for seven minutes about it, letting your mind take you where it wants to go.

_____

_____

_____

_____

_____

_____

_____

— Day Two

Write about how what you read today builds on what you read yesterday. If you're reading fiction, what new plot points did you notice? What character motivations became clearer? If you're reading nonfiction, what ideas are being developed? How do you think about those ideas now that you've read more?

_____

_____

_____

_____

_____

— Day Three

Write as though you are explaining what you read today to a five-year-old.

_____

_____

_____

_____

_____

— Day Four

Pick a location that is related to your reading—a fantasy place, a building, a city, a continent, a rainforest, a library, a house of worship, or a home. Write about how that location informs the story or the context of the content you're reading.

_____

_____

_____

_____

_____

— Day Five

Reflect on how your mind is doing with this deep reading practice. Is it easier or more difficult than you expected? Are you noticing that you are able to retain what you are reading? What did you get out of this week's reading? Are you able not to take a strong position but simply to enjoy learning more? Why or why not?

_____

_____

_____

_____

_____

THREE KINDS OF "DOING"

Adding Experiences to Thinking

(WORTH REPEATING)

BRIEF

Imagine reading a recipe. Now picture taking a test about how to make it. You'll answer questions about how many cups and teaspoons of flour, sugar, and baking soda are required to bake that cake, for example. You'll have to answer process questions like how to mix the ingredients, what temperature to use for baking, and how many minutes the mixture ought to bake. Even if you memorized every ingredient, each quantity, and all the steps, would you know what the cake tasted like? Experience adds depth to reading. Experience is the difference between knowing about something and knowing it more intimately—with more of yourself.

This activity gives you a chance to deepen your understanding of a topic that you are reading about right now. Whether you're reading a novel or a nonfiction book, you can access more of it through direct, indirect, or imaginative experiences.

ACTIVITY AND JOURNAL

Here are a few ways to add experience to your reading.

Direct experience: If you're reading about cooking, building, quilting, computer programming, or gaming, the best way to deepen your relationship to the topic is to participate in it. You can *do* the activity to experience it firsthand.

What's an activity you have only read about?

_____

If you're stuck trying to think of an activity, here are a few suggestions that might get the ball rolling:

- Baking a particular recipe you haven't tried before
- Playing a new board or video game
- Acting (memorizing lines and then acting them out)
- Learning to knit
- Growing African violets

- Painting a landscape
- Calculating square footage
- Gardening
- Playing sudoku or Wordle
- Zip-lining
- Climbing at an indoor gym
- Building a bonfire

Make a plan to try this activity. You don't have to do it well, but give yourself enough time to experience it. Make a plan. Acquire the materials. Read the directions. Pick a day to *do* the activity. You might need more than a day. After you feel you've experienced the activity, reflect on the difference between what you thought the experience would be like and what it *actually* was like once you did it.

_____

_____

Indirect experience: Sometimes we can't do the thing we read about. For instance, you can't visit a historical era. (It's over!) Perhaps you aren't interested in making pad thai from scratch. Maybe you don't want to learn how to play the drums. You can enjoy an indirect experience instead. You might watch a movie that is set in a historical period. You might eat at a Thai restaurant where someone else prepares the food for you. You can go to a rock concert and listen to a drum solo.

Indirect experiences often rely on the expertise of others. If you watch a movie set in a particular time period, one director's interpretation may be different than another's. Indirect experiences benefit from repetition. This is how someone becomes a chocolate connoisseur or a movie critic. By indirectly experiencing similar content repeatedly, you develop the ability to evaluate the quality of the item or experience. Indirect experiences give you the chance to deepen your knowledge of a particular topic by including the expertise of others.

What's an indirect experience you've had that helped you expand your understanding of a topic? How did it deepen your understanding? Is there an area of interest in your life where you feel you've had sufficient indirect experiences to qualify as someone who can judge the quality of that topic? For instance, you know enough about golf from watching it again and again that you can tell which players are really good versus those who are average.

_____

_____

_____

Imagination: A third way you add experience to your learning is by using your imagination! One of the most powerful ways to use your imagination is through participation in theater. Inhabiting a character who has a different perspective and personality from your own allows you to have a vicarious experience of an alternate worldview without rendering judgment on it. You allow yourself to consider which habits of thought formed this character's motivations and choices. By inhabiting this character's world through pretending to be that character, you catch a glimpse of possible motivations and conditions that explain that person's choices.

We also enter our imaginations when we read fiction. Historical fiction is particularly powerful because it filters factual content through the perspectives of fictional characters we come to know intimately. The author sketches the setting for us and then plants the characters in that world, helping us imagine how the context impacted the people who lived at that time. Historical fiction helps humanize the dates and events of the past.

Lastly, we can visit historical sites or landmarks as a way to enrich our imaginations for a past time. Our visits help us refine the imagery that we hold in our minds as we think about other times and places. Remember, imagery informs how we think as much as words. A visit to a particular place that is known for its historical significance is a powerful way to add depth to your thinking.

Consider the ways you use your imagination now to help you gain access to other experiences and viewpoints. As a small child, you might have used dress-up clothes and play to experience life from a different perspective. Remember pretending to be a dog by crawling on the floor and lapping up water from a dish? By middle school, a lot of kids shift their energy to writing fan fiction, giving new storylines to well-loved characters. In that spirit, here's one additional idea: for a week, keep a diary pretending to be a historical person or a fictional character from a historical era. Allow yourself to include the social, political, and economic factors that influence decisions that person makes. Use the space below to decide which sort of experience you intend to have this week. Feel free to use this space for that diary if you'd like.

_____

_____

_____

_____

_____

_____

_____

BREAK THE RULES

Overturning Expectations to Force an Encounter

(WORTH REPEATING)

BRIEF

You've read, and you've experienced, but have you *encountered*? On your quest to think well, one of the most powerful tools in your kit is the one that knocks you off your feet! I call it an "encounter." An encounter destabilizes you. An encounter is the overwhelm that overturns. It's the grizzly bear that lopes into view while you're out hiking what you thought was a safe trail for humans. It's the first time someone puts a violin in your hands and asks you to make music. It's choosing to be friends with someone from another culture, language, or religion. An encounter lets you know, in that moment, that all the resources you currently have will not make you skillful in meeting this new challenge. An encounter shifts how you know and what you know.

Consider this example. It's one thing to *read* about a video game. You might learn all the rules, how to level up in the game, and what keeps your character alive. You might add the *experience* of watching the game played by an expert player via livestream. You might jeer at the player for making what you see as boneheaded moves. Your understanding of the game might be top-notch, and you might be able to analyze why the choices this player makes don't work or were poorly executed. An *encounter* with the game, however, occurs the first time *you* play it. Suddenly you're thrust into the high-speed decision-making and deft finger manipulation necessary to play well. When you enter the game as a participant, you're forced into situations you couldn't anticipate otherwise. What you *know* doesn't translate into the *skill* it takes to play well. You have to grow your skills over time—through playing, not just through reading about the game and watching someone else play.

An encounter is the most pivotal of all the critical thinking tools. It may not deliver detailed analysis or provide you with a comprehensive list of facts, but it thrusts you into challenging your limited perspective. You will become immediately aware of what *you still don't know*. Encounters provoke reevaluation of what you thought you knew or understood. That's the differentiating force of an encounter.

ACTIVITY

One way to create an encounter with a familiar activity is to "break the rules." By going against the established patterns, you generate new insight into how the activity was designed and why. Let's try breaking the rules in a familiar game. Have you ever deliberately broken the rules of a game you play? For instance, if you were to play chess and you changed the way the pieces move, how much does that alter your strategy or gum up the objective of the game? One way to get to the inside of our own thinking is to break its habits—to rearrange the furniture in our minds so we have a different view.

In this activity, you're going to mess up a game that has a specific set of rules and then evaluate the impact of that change. Try any of these activities and then use the journal space to write about what you discovered.

1. **SCORING:** Change the points system of a game like basketball. For instance, create a shot worth four points and another worth half a point. Consider subtracting points when someone commits a foul. Any other rules you'd like to change or add? Get a friend to play a quick game using the new scoring system. How do these changes alter the strategy of the game? For you? For your opponent?

2. **GAMEPLAY:** Play a card game where the top five cards in the draw pile are always visible. What do you do differently in order to win? How do you protect yourself from your opponent's strategy?

3. **PIECE MOVEMENT:** Alter how the pieces move in chess. What happens if the knight can move up three squares before moving right or left? What if

the queen is not allowed to move horizontally, but only vertically? What if the king can move two squares at a time rather than one? Make up any changes you'd like. Play a match with one change. Now play a match with two or more changes. What happens? How is game play impacted?

4. **CHEATING:** Find cheat codes for an online game you love. How does knowing the codes help you understand the game differently from before you knew the cheat codes?

JOURNAL

Record the new rules of your game.

_____

_____

_____

_____

_____

_____

Free-write a bit about what you learned when you broke the rules of a game. What new questions did you consider about the design of the original game? Note any strategy adjustments you made for the new rules. Lastly, consider how rule-breaking helps you understand the original construction of the game—why it is played the way it is.

_____

_____

_____

PERSPECTIVE-TAKING AND TOLERANCE

Deconstructing Familiar Stories

(WORTH REPEATING)

BRIEF

Encounters force us to reevaluate what we assumed was true for everyone. If you are used to wearing shoes indoors, for example, you'll be in for a surprise when you visit a family whose practice is to remove their shoes before entering the interior of their house. If you are used to eating with a fork and knife from your own plate, it might startle you to be invited to dinner where the family shares a common dish, and you use your right hand with a piece of bread to scoop up your portion of the meal. When we confront difference, we have two jobs: to be curious about the perspective of the other person and to learn to tolerate our discomfort (that knee-jerk reaction that says, "This is nonsense!").

It takes time to grow this skill of setting aside our comfortable ways of knowing and being open to accepting difference. Acceptance and agreement are not the same. You might learn to accept that taking off your shoes to keep the living space of a home clean is a reasonable idea and still not adopt it for yourself in your own house. Understanding the perspective of another person does not require agreement. Likewise, you can accept a difference even while you feel uncomfortable with it. You might not like eating with your hands. You can notice your discomfort and still respect the other culture's habits. This is what it means to be "tolerant." You're not tolerating the other person or their perspective; you're tolerating *your* discomfort with the difference between how they are in the world and how you are.

ACTIVITY

One way to unearth alternate perspectives is to ask better questions. Start with a significant national narrative for your home country. For the United States, the founding of our country is a popular place to begin. Take a second look at the story. It's helpful to identify as many possible narrators as you can. Think back to *The True Story of the 3 Little Pigs* in Part One, Lesson Two. What other viewpoints can you identify that you may or may not know yet? The following questions are designed to address the founding of the United States but can be tweaked for any national story you want to revisit.

ASK: *Who's telling this version of the story? Who are the major players?*

FOLLOW UP: *Who isn't named in this version of the story? What do we know about them? (These would be people who are not necessarily famous or frequently included in the narrative you know.)*

WONDER: *What were the goals of the original explorers? Who had the authority to commission the settlement of North America? Who recognizes that authority, and who doesn't?*

ASK: *What was the mission of the first settlers? Who benefited, and who didn't?*

CONSIDER: *Who decides which people are heroes, using what criteria? Who decides which people are villains, using what criteria?*

ASK: *Whose voice is ignored in this story? Whose voice is amplified?*

WONDER: *What is the underlying value being promoted in this version of the story? By whom? What is good about that value? What is limiting about it?*

_____

_____

_____

_____

_____

In addition to viewpoint questions, monitor your reactions—tolerate your discomfort as you unearth new information.

WONDER: _What do you hope is true? Why do you hope that?_

CONSIDER: _What are you afraid might be the truth? Why do you fear that version of the story?_

ASK: _How does the familiar version of the story affirm or harm your self-concept?_

CHECK IN: _Do you notice any body sensations or emotions now? What are they?_

CONNECT: _What do you think caused that sensation or emotion? How do you explain it?_

_____

_____

_____

_____

_____

JOURNAL

In addition to examining a story by imagining different perspectives, getting to know someone who holds a very different viewpoint or life experience is another great way to provoke an encounter. Consider meeting an expert, a person from a different religious background, someone from another country, a member of a rival sports team, or a war veteran. Ask them viewpoint questions about their experiences, and journal what you learned.

_____

_____

_____

_____

_____

_____

_____

_____

_____

_____

COFFEEHOUSE CONVERSATIONS

Eavesdropping on the Table Next to You

(WORTH REPEATING)

BRIEF

Sometimes we spend so much time in our own communities, we forget that other people organize how they understand reality from a radically different point of view. One way to expand your awareness of others is to deliberately eavesdrop on conversations around you! Your mission is to listen to what people at a nearby table say. They may simply exchange information, order a drink, or make a phone call you can't hear. After some time, however, you may notice that you can hear a conversation— an exchange of several sentences back and forth. What are they saying? Can you learn anything from them?

In this next activity, the goal is to simply notice and listen without inserting yourself into the discussion. If you can go to a part of town that is unfamiliar to you, you may be more stimulated by the differences—or even the surprising-to-you similarities!

ACTIVITY

Pick a coffeehouse that's not in your neighborhood. Bring your laptop or a small notebook and pen. Make yourself comfortable, and plan to sit at the table for at least an hour. Sit with your back to a wall so you can see the majority of the room. This posture also allows you to type or take notes without someone reading over your shoulder.

Part of your visit will be filled with ambient noise and bits of dialogue. Allow your mind to tune into the words and exchanges you overhear. Jot them in your notebook or on your laptop. You can write down a snippet of conversation, a word pair, an interesting remark, a turn of phrase you don't use, an attitude, or a full-on dialogue that goes back and forth, if you hear it and can capture it.

You may or may not have any earth-shattering revelations with this activity, but the idea is to stay curious and attentive to what *other people say*. This practice is also ideal for writing believable dialogue in fiction and getting out of your own stereotypes about how people talk and think.

JOURNAL

What did you learn in this activity? Is it one you'd like to try again? Which overheard terms or ideas felt new to you? Which felt utterly ordinary and familiar? Can you explain why? Learning to listen well is a discipline that is really useful in critical thinking. Sometimes while we're listening, we actually tune out what is being said while we plan what we want to say back! By learning how to sit quietly to take copious notes of what other people are saying, you are teaching yourself to be observant, attentive, and accurate!

_____

_____

_____

_____

_____

_____

_____

ONE MEMORY, TWO STORIES

Comparing Notes about a Shared Memory

(WORTH REPEATING)

BRIEF

Have you ever gotten into an argument with someone about *what really happened* at an event where you were both present? When two people experience the same event, they don't always remember the same details! There are good reasons for those differences, too. Our minds are crafty. They sort details based on what helps us feel right-side-up with the world, not so much based on what is accurate to objective reality. Part of thinking well is taking the time to consider more perspectives than the one you hold—to imagine that different people will recall and interpret the same circumstances through different lenses. Most of us remember the parts of an event that had a direct impact on our own experience. We may overlook what was going on for the other person or people in the same place at the same time.

ACTIVITY

This activity will give you a chance to compare notes with someone who was at the same place with you, at the same time.

1. Divide a sheet of paper into three sections, as if you were folding it to fit in a long envelope. Title each section with the name of three different events that form a part of your personal or family history. Choose events

that you remember—not something that happened when you were a baby or an event that has been told to you but that you don't recall directly. Select memories that involve a person you know who can be easily reached for comment. Events that might work well include the following:

- Memorable holiday celebrations

- Vacation moments (either fabulous or disastrous ones)

- Unexpected obstacles that you had to overcome

- A "first" experience, like when you rode a roller coaster or broke your arm

- A time you got in big trouble

- An accident (car, bike, gymnastics, rock climbing . . .)

> ***Pro tip:***
> If you're struggling to choose an event, flip through photos on your phone or in an old photo album. A picture can spark the return of a memory you've forgotten!

2. For each event, write about what happened on your folded paper. Try to describe it from start to finish, pretending that someone who doesn't know you will be reading your story to understand it. Get into free-writing mode, letting the words hit the page without worrying about spelling or grammar, and write as much as you can remember without stopping. The best events to use for this exercise are experiences that you remember, not the ones that everyone retells each time you get together. Those retold experiences become a "family-accepted version" and prevent deviations in memory.

3. Select one event. Find somebody in your life who remembers the event. This person may be a family member or friend. Pick a memory you have that you haven't confirmed with other participants. For instance, you might remember living through an earthquake when you were seven years old. What is the memory your brother had of the same earthquake?

4. Ask the person you chose to tell you their memory of the same event by asking an open question like, "Grandpa, do you remember the time we ran out of gas on the highway? Can you tell me what you remember about what happened?" Express only the bare bones of the event without telling your full version to avoid influencing their version. Take notes, or record the interview using your cell phone. Pay attention to which parts of their story are different from your own.

5. Fold another sheet of paper in half lengthwise to make two columns. Jot down the similarities in your stories in one column and the differences in the other.

6. Craft a summary of the event, including what you learned in the interview. Highlight what your two stories have in common and what is different about them. You might notice details that contradict each other, too. Then use the journal prompts to conduct some analysis.

_____

_____

_____

_____

_____

_____

_____

_____

JOURNAL

Because so much of critical thinking is rooted in self-awareness, let's take a look at how your body and mind reacted to the other person's version of the event you selected.

- As you interviewed the other person, what were you hoping you'd hear? Confirmation of the details or a different version? Why do you think that is?

- As you listened to their version, were you accepting of their version or resistant? Did you want to interrupt to correct their story? Why or why not?

- Were you impatient to tell your version of the same event to this other person, or did you find it easy to sit back and listen? How do you understand your reaction?

_____

_____

_____

_____

_____

- Now that you have noticed your own reaction, what happened when you told your slightly different version to this other person?

- Did the other person accept your version or refute it? How did that feel?

- Did you interrupt their refutation of your version? If so, why? Did you try to correct their memory? What did you say? Did you argue with each other, or were you respectful of the differences?

- What was at stake in each retelling? Who benefited from each version, and who didn't?

- Did the two of you merge your memories to create a new, more complete story? Why or why not? How was that for you?

- Did either of you feel the need to persuade the other person that their memory was off? What was that like? Did the persuasion tactic work, or did it make either of you feel defensive of your own versions? Why do you think that is? Did any blanks or misunderstandings get cleared up? Which ones?

- How do you understand the event now? Did you change any of your memories to match the new information? Why or why not?

- Did your interpretation of the meaning of the memory change at all? How?

_____

_____

_____

_____

_____

As you can see, the practice of noticing how we respond to someone else holding a slightly different view of the same event is at the root of our thinking skills. It takes practice to listen to someone double down on their memories when you remember a slightly (or radically) different story. This difference in how we turn our memories into stories applies equally well to how we form our beliefs. Journal for a few minutes about what you learned about yourself in this process. Are you curious or defensive? Are you more interested in persuading someone else to accept your way of seeing things, or are you open to having your ideas or memories challenged or reshaped? Why do you think that is?

_____

_____

_____

_____

_____

_____

_____

_____

_____

_____

_____

_____

CLEAN COMMUNICATION

Experimenting with Dissent

(WORTH REPEATING)

BRIEF

In the last activity, you experimented with inviting dissent into a conversation with you. The memory you double-checked with a friend or relative gave you a chance to see a few things: 1) memories are not reliably the same for each person in the same experience, 2) we create stories from our memories to help us hold them, and 3) our interpretations usually favor us. One of the feelings that surfaces when someone challenges the story you tell with an alternate version is invalidation. Most of us dislike being invalidated. Invalidation is literally a challenge to the validity of our ideas, beliefs, memories, opinions, and identity. Another way to think about invalidation, though, is to consider the alternative viewpoint as dissent.

I like to say, "Dissent is the chlorine in the pool." Dissent keeps groups healthy and free of algae (or other bad things). What is dissent, you ask? Dissent is the choice by a group member to break with the group's accepted logic story. For instance, if you come from a family of meat eaters and you decide to become a vegetarian, you're dissenting through your actions. Sometimes dissent is fairly benign—you prefer an Android phone in a family of iPhone users. Sometimes dissent is expressed as remembering a shared experience with a different interpretation of why it happened the way it did. Sometimes your dissenting beliefs create waves of controversy and concern in your family if, for example, you hold a different religious belief or political view.

Becoming skilled at dissenting while preserving your relationships is an art! Too often, when we dissent, the other person feels judged (they see your viewpoint as an invalidation of theirs) or you feel at risk of exclusion (your perspective is seen as toxic or dangerous to the group). This next activity is meant to support you in learning to dissent as well as you can—keeping your side of the street clean. You may not be able to prevent your parents or best friends from worry, but that's okay. The key is learning how to distinguish between your love for your people and your need (and right) to think differently for yourself at this time in your life. It's also important to learn to give that same respect and curiosity to the people in your world who risk sharing their dissenting views with you.

ACTIVITY

To begin, identify one way of thinking you hold that does not align with that of someone in your life whom you value. You might start with a perspective that is not an earthquake of difference. For instance, perhaps you don't agree with your parents' perspective on your musical tastes or video game preferences. Maybe you want to take up a risky sport like urban gymnastics or be an exchange student even though your family has never traveled abroad. These are low-stakes dissents. High-stakes dissent would be tied to politics, religion, identity, and sexuality.

1. Identify a belief or value you hold that someone you are close to does not hold.

   _____

2. What do you wish the other person understood about your position?

   _____

3. Which facts, anecdotes, and experiences support your way of thinking?

   _____

   _____

4. Which facts, anecdotes, and experiences support the other person's way of thinking?

    _____

    _____

5. What's the biggest obstacle you feel you must overcome to help the other person understand your way of thinking?

    _____

6. What is the primary difference of opinion the other person has shared with you?

    _____

7. Imagine how a respectful conversation between yourself and the other person might go. Use phrases like "I believe . . ." and "I'm curious to hear what you think and why . . ."

Next, draft a conversation between you and the other person that represents your views and their beliefs as accurately as you can. Notice when you tend toward minimizing the other person's perspective, or when you get snarky or insistent. Back up and rewrite if necessary, doing your best to get inside how the other person may be thinking.

CONVERSATION: *Using the lines below, fill in the blanks for your dialogue.*

You: _____

The other party: _____

You: _____

The other party: _____

You: _____

The other party: _____

You: _____

The other party: _____

You: _____

The other party: _____

JOURNAL

If you dare, bring this conversation to the other person and ask for feedback. Did you accurately represent their views? How do they feel reading your viewpoint? Then write about what you learned in this process. What was the most difficult aspect to incorporate in your dialogue: the reasonableness of the other person, or putting forth your view in a clear, concise, non-attacking manner? You might also like to use the space provided to explore how holding a different view feels in your relationship and what you can do to create a better dynamic between you. Write about this experience.

_____

_____

_____

_____

_____

_____

Part Three

THE APPLICATION: LEARNING THE ART OF INTERPRETATION

THE BODY INVENTORY

Developing Self-Awareness

(WORTH REPEATING)

BRIEF

Our bodies and minds work fast. We make involuntary snap judgments the second we meet someone. We size up their hairstyle, their clothing, the way they stand, the volume of their voice, and bam! We draw a conclusion: I trust you, or I don't trust you.

Sometimes you're chatting along, enjoying a conversation, and then your conversation partner stuns you with an opinion you don't hold. Your body sends a message of shock to your system—one that you try to keep off of your face in order to hide your discomfort. The same thing happens to you when you go to study any subject, whether a controversial issue or merely a period in history. A self-aware thinker notices how they are triggered by the topic; they might get defensive, anxious, smug, self-righteous, and more. For this activity, pick a topic that provokes a quick reaction in your body.

In order to learn the art of interpretation (understanding texts, viewpoints, opinions, research, and data), we begin with the art of self-awareness—noticing what happens in our bodies.

ACTIVITY

This activity is designed to help you investigate a specific topic for study. If you are about to write a paper for school or you have a desire to learn more about a particular topic to understand it better, select that topic for this activity.

Topic:

_____

— Before Study

Before studying the topic, ask yourself: when you think of your topic, what happens in your body? Check all that apply:

☐ Do you feel a tightness in your jaw or stomach?

☐ Are you relaxed and at ease?

☐ Are you nervous or bracing yourself?

☐ Are you sweating?

☐ Alternatively, is there no physical sensation?

Next, let's evaluate the thoughts you have.

• Identify vocabulary related to the topic. Make a list, with or without definitions.

_____   _____

_____   _____

_____   _____

_____   _____

• List slogans and sayings, for all viewpoints, related to the topic.

_____

_____

_____

_____

_____

- Note prejudgments you make about people—both the people who agree with you and those who don't.

_____

_____

_____

_____

- Name your hunch. What about your current viewpoint would make life better for everyone if they adopted it?

_____

_____

_____

_____

Now you're ready to study your topic. Take a few days to read and reflect.

— After Study

After you've studied your topic, read through the previous list again and note any changes or additional information. For instance, as you studied, how did your body respond to the information? You might notice when you felt surprised or confirmed, when you got bored, when you wanted to rush through what you were reading, or when you noticed a thrill of agreement or the irritation of having a belief challenged or overturned.

Ask yourself these questions:

- What provoked your body's reactions? Can you tie what you learned to specific emotions like fear, worry, anger, delight, or vindication? Can you identify the source of the emotion?

_____

_____

_____

- Was your initial vocabulary list representative of what you read or learned? What new words can be added to your understanding of this topic? What terms took on a different meaning from the one you thought you knew?

_____

_____

_____

- How do you see the prejudgments and hunches you identified earlier now? Any modifications you'd like to make?

_____

_____

_____

Next, ask yourself these questions:

- What insights ("aha" moments, new thoughts, or provocative questions) have you generated?

  _____

  _____

- How do your insights alter what you understood about the topic before you began?

  _____

  _____

- What new questions do you have?

  _____

  _____

- Have you vetted the information for CACAO (currency, accuracy, coverage, authority, and objectivity; see Part One, Lesson Ten)? Did the research you conducted account for each of the items from the CACAO rubric?

C _____

A _____

C _____

A _____

O _____

JOURNAL

Your body isn't necessarily a reliable arbiter of truth. Sometimes you react based on stereotypes or past traumatic experiences. That said, your body is an excellent tuning fork for understanding your reactions to ideas and information you consume. Noticing what your body tells you, not just what your mind thinks, is essential in developing the self-awareness needed for quality thinking! When you notice smugness, for instance, you can learn to slow down and deliberately consider what you're reading rather than skimming over it. When you feel anxious, you can ask yourself what's at stake in the reading, identify it, and then set it aside temporarily in order to read the material more dispassionately.

Use the following journal space to reflect on how you've begun to notice the way your body contributes to your thoughts. Identify defensiveness, self-righteousness, and irritation. These are clues to the thinking you have yet to do!

_____

_____

_____

_____

_____

_____

_____

_____

FRAMING THE ARGUMENT

The Power of Context in Persuasion

(WORTH REPEATING)

BRIEF

Have you ever gone to an art museum? Have you noticed that sometimes the frames are even more elaborate than the paintings? Frames enhance the way we receive artwork. The frame gives the viewer a hint about a painting's elegance, importance, style, or aesthetic, and how it fits with other paintings in the same room. The best frames highlight the artwork itself, enhancing it. The worst frames detract from the story the painter wants to tell.

The same concept applies to how we come to know information. Remember the activity where you examined headlines and chyrons (Part One, Lesson Eight)? These act as frames for the information being delivered in the same space. Similarly, the way a book is bound delivers a subliminal message about its importance, elegance, or value. For example, a book with gilded edges and a leather cover conveys authority. A paperback novel appears consumable and less important.

Another means of seeing a subject's frame is through the way the information is delivered to you. The frame for a subject might be the *perspective* of an instructor, the impersonal objectivity of a textbook, or the carefully researched opinions found in an academic journal. The frame might be a historical novel or the nightly news story on television. The frame may be the vehicle of delivery (the style of artwork on the book cover, a documentary in color or black and white, an audio versus a print text, or a glossy brochure). One way to get beyond the seductive power of the frame is to name it and identify how it steers your first impressions.

ACTIVITY

Select a source of information. What kind of frame is being used for this information?

- Is the source a human being? If so, what about this person shapes your reaction? Their style of dress? Their hair? Their voice? Is the person in a position of authority or a close friend? Is the person expressing firsthand experiences or reporting what someone else experienced? Does the person have the credentials to speak with authority? What credentials? What about the person causes you to either trust them implicitly or react with initial distrust? Note these qualities.

_____

_____

_____

_____

- Does the frame reference an authority figure? Someone with qualifications? Someone with direct experience? God? A celebrity? A political leader? A religious leader? A PhD?

_____

_____

_____

_____

- If the source is material, what's the packaging? A sturdy book? Are the pages of the book edged in gold or roughly cut? Is it a paperback? What's the cover design? Is a credentialed expert prominently featured on the packaging? Who is the publisher, or is it self-published?

_____

_____

_____

- If the source is digital or media, is it a website for an advocacy group? Is it a multimedia presentation? An interview with a firsthand witness? A collection of handwritten letters? A TED Talk? A radio show? An audio recording? A historic fragment from an archaeological dig?

_____

_____

_____

- How does the framing impact you? Do you see it as reliable or credible? Why?

_____

_____

_____

- What could cause you to either lose trust in its reliability or gain it? Can you compare it to other similar sources (websites featuring different viewpoints, books on the same topic, audio versus print version, comparable television stations)? How does that comparison impact your emotional reaction to the source? Which sources appear trustworthy, and which don't? Why?

_____

_____

_____

_____

_____

- What does this frame imply or hope to elicit? Check all that apply.

  ☐ Objectivity   ☐ Awe

  ☐ Emotional connection   ☐ Empathy

  ☐ Reflection   ☐ Credibility

  ☐ Outrage   ☐ Protest

  ☐ Respect

  ☐ Something else: _____

- Does the frame support the status quo (how things are currently), or does it challenge it (showing how things could be instead)? For instance, if it's a petition, the goal is to create change. If the book is an exposé, it intends to upend the established narrative. If it's a report, the goal may be to affirm established findings.

_____

_____

JOURNAL

Go to a bookcase in your house or the library. Without thinking about the topics or titles, select books based on how their "frames"—their covers, bindings, and spines—appear to you. Stack them according to these categories:

- Authoritative and trustworthy

- Pleasure reading

- Instruction

- Humor

- Persuasion

Can you tell from the designs, bindings, and fonts how you are meant to think about the contents before you even read the books? What did you learn from this exercise?

_____

_____

_____

_____

_____

RADICAL DIFFERENCE

Choosing to Honor Another Perspective

(WORTH REPEATING)

BRIEF

I love my friends. I love my family. I bet you love yours, too. One of the ways we show our love for our people is through loyalty. We tell each other that we'll stand with one another "through thick and thin." What we mean is that no matter what the other person is going through, they can count on us to be helpful and kind, supportive and trustworthy. We tend to believe our own people—their stories, their claims, their sources of authority, and their way of seeing the world. We'll defend them against critics. Sometimes we even choose to give up our own interpretations of an experience just so we can fit in with our favorite people.

Even though allegiance to our people is natural and often valuable, it carries with it a danger, too. Our loyalty to our loved ones sometimes makes us critical of people who are outside of our community. We're suspicious of outsiders and too trusting of insiders. Quality thinking requires your mind to dispassionately consider a variety of interpretations of the same information from multiple sources. I like to call this the "academic disposition." You choose to be calm, nonreactive, and open to alternative ways of thinking about a topic. You stay curious about challenges to the way you have been conditioned to think.

To help achieve this disposition, try "accepting radical difference." It works like this: Go into any course of study on the hunt for ways the writer or researcher shows up as radically different from your preconceptions. Be deliberately curious. Note when a contradiction to your beliefs surfaces and then high-five yourself for noticing and noting it. Accepting radical difference is not the same as "conversion." Instead, you're making room for these other ideas to pull up an armchair next to yours, to sit for a conversation over chips and salsa.

ACTIVITY

Select an article about a controversial topic written by someone with whom you disagree. If you're in an especially daring mood, pick one written by someone you automatically dismiss or discount. You'll be observing their "logic story" for their beliefs. (Remember, a logic story is the community's explanation of why their beliefs make sense. It doesn't necessarily mean that their story is factual or true in the scientific sense. Sometimes it is a matter of community practice or identity that creates the logic for why their view makes the most sense.)

Instructions

1. Print the article.

2. Go through the article with a highlighter. Highlight any statement, term, or idea that contradicts what you and your community believe. Each time you highlight, jot down the essential idea in the space below:

_____

_____

_____

_____

_____

_____

3. Next to each idea, add the reason the writer proposes for why that idea makes sense. Resist the temptation to explain it away or to judge it. Get *inside* the idea enough to represent it.

For example, let's say you are from a religious tradition that doesn't have any food restrictions. Perhaps you chose to read about a religion that does. You will highlight the restrictions and then go through each of the restrictions and use the logic of the writer to justify that restriction.

Or say you and your community love watching professional American football and believe that it includes an acceptable amount of risk to the health of the players. To challenge your opinion, you choose to read an article by a researcher who has data about the long-term effects of concussions. The writer argues that American football at the professional level is too dangerous and should be banned. You note the data and conclusions this researcher offers. Then you write a brief explanation for each point that shows how this researcher used that data to form those interpretations.

Your goal is not to agree. It's to understand better how this other person from a different community interprets the world differently from how you and yours do.

JOURNAL

Did you ever think about the fact that the people in your life are as persuaded by the logic of their communities as you are by yours? Accepting radical difference is one way to engage with other communities. You can use the respectful stance of "wonder" to explore what others believe without feeling threatened. Use this space to wonder, writing your own questions that arose as you explored this other viewpoint.

_____

_____

_____

_____

MOVIE REVIEWS

Using the Same Material for Opposing Takes

(ONE TIME)

BRIEF

Have you ever noticed that two people can watch the same movie and come to completely different conclusions about whether or not it was a good film? One movie reviewer might comment on how realistic the setting appeared, while another reviewer might say, "The scenery felt forced and inauthentic." How can two reviewers watching identical content draw such drastically different conclusions about the same film?

In this activity, you get to watch a movie! Then you'll read reviews other people wrote about the film, isolating the features they use to present their arguments to you. Your task is to identify how they justify their celebration of the content or their judgments, whichever the case may be. By the end, you may notice that your views of the film shift to align more forcefully with the viewpoint you already hold, or you may find that your feelings about the film change! That's the goal: noticing how our opinions are formed and influenced.

ACTIVITY

Select a movie to watch. You can pick a movie you have already seen and love, a movie you've never seen, or a film you watched and hated. It's helpful if the film is from within the last several years in order to find the most up-to-date reviews.

Watch or rewatch the film. Then determine if you like the movie or not.

Next, head to the review site Rotten Tomatoes (rottentomatoes.com). A healthy red tomato icon next to a reviewer's comments means that the reviewer likes the film. A green splat means the reviewer didn't like the film. Select a review bearing each type of tomato, red and green.

Read a review that agrees with your perspective. Notice the elements that the reviewer highlights as evidence for their perspective. Check the boxes for elements this reviewer mentioned:

☐ Acting by one or more actors

☐ Screenplay/dialogue

☐ Sets, costumes, makeup

☐ Storyline (compelling or not)

☐ Special effects

☐ Directing

☐ Comparisons to other films

☐ Other: _____

Now read the opposing view, either a green splat for a reviewer who disliked the film or a red tomato for someone who did. Go through the list of characteristics again, and check the boxes for the elements that this reviewer uses to support their perspective.

☐ Acting by one or more actors

☐ Screenplay/dialogue

☐ Sets, costumes, makeup

☐ Storyline (compelling or not)

☐ Special effects

☐ Directing

☐ Comparisons to other films

☐ Other: _____

Now that you've read two very different views of the film, ask yourself how you felt as you read the one that challenged your perspective.

- Did you feel defensive?

_____

- Did you find yourself thinking of justifications for your perspective? If so, what were they?

_____

_____

- Was there any point that made you reconsider your own perspective? What was it?

_____

Now that you've read reviews *after* watching a film, reverse the strategy and read the reviews *before* you watch a film.

Which film will you watch?

_____

Think about how the reviews predispose your viewpoint. For instance, before watching the film, ask yourself these questions:

- Which review did I find more compelling? Do I feel inclined to like or dislike the movie before I even watch it?

_____

- What am I expecting to like?

_____

- What am I expecting to dislike?

_____

JOURNAL

After the film is over, compare your experience of the film to what you expected to feel. There are no right answers. In fact, the best work you can do is to notice how you were influenced by what you read before you saw the movie and how your experience differed or aligned with those reviews. You might also reflect on how differently you felt about the reviews, reading them after you watched a movie as compared to reading them before. Each of these experiences is a window into how you form your reactions in every encounter with people and ideas.

A bonus activity: watch multiple films telling the same story. Many classic works of literature have several movie adaptations. Comparing the choices of directors, actors, and screenplay writers is another way to recognize how we each bring our own interpretations to similar information. Use this journaling space to make those comparisons.

_____

_____

_____

_____

_____

_____

_____

_____

A LENS
WITH A VIEW

Finding a Different Perspective

(ONE TIME)

BRIEF

The art of seeing is at the center of thinking well. Perhaps you hold an opinion because the issue at stake directly impacts you and your community. You are *up close* to the way the issue plays out because it is directly related to your life. Imagine, for instance, being a person who uses a wheelchair (in fact, perhaps you do). You will have important opinions about ease of access to any building based on your direct experience of using a wheelchair.

Sometimes we are at a distance from an issue and hold an opinion anyway. When an issue is *remote* and doesn't impact us directly, we are more likely to take a stand with less careful scrutiny of the issues involved. It's easier to be rigid, in fact, when you know *less* about a topic. There's a kind of clarity that comes from seeing less and reducing the topic to the parts that make you feel comfortable.

One way to work with the art of seeing is to practice shifting your view deliberately. Instead of focusing on abstract topics, let's use your eyes to test the power of adjusting the lens of perspective.

ACTIVITY

You'll need a few tools for this activity, so take some time to collect them. Alternatively, you may need to *go* somewhere where the tool lives, like an observatory for the telescope. Here's what you'll need:

- Magnifying glass
- Binoculars
- Telescope

These are all tools of sight. They each alter the way your eyes see. The magnifying glass allows your eyes to boost their power to see a bit better. The microscope lets you see what is invisible to the naked eye. Binoculars draw in images that are far away, making them seem closer than they really are. A telescope brings celestial items into a clear view despite being thousands and millions of miles away.

When you have your tools collected, first use your natural vision to look at an item in the list below. Then, one at a time, use the sight-boosting tools to examine the same item. You'll record your notes about what you missed in your first view that became clearer with a boosted view.

— Magnifying Glass

Begin with your naked eye. Look at each of the items in the following list, and jot notes about what you see. Then look at the same item again with a magnifying glass. What else do you see that you missed before? Jot that down as well. Notice additional variations in the color, edges, structural elements, and depth or breadth of contours. Use the columns to take notes for each.

OBJECT	WITH YOUR EYES	WITH A MAGNIFYING GLASS
Bug (ladybug, ant, moth, dead fly or bee)		
Leaf		
Strand of hair		

OBJECT	WITH YOUR EYES	WITH A MAGNIFYING GLASS
Strawberry		
Pencil shavings		
Old coins		

— Microscope

If you have a microscope, you will have a great time with the next part of this activity. Remember, look at the item with your naked eye first and then look through the microscope. The differences will be even more dramatic than what you saw with a magnifying glass.

OBJECT	WITH YOUR EYES	WITH A MICROSCOPE
Strand of hair		
Salt		
Onion skin		
Cheek cells (scrape the inside of your cheek with a popscile stick and apply it to a clean slide)		
Spiderweb		

OBJECT	WITH YOUR EYES	WITH A MICROSCOPE
Feather		
Earwax		
Flower petal		

— Binoculars

Now it's time to leave home and head somewhere with a view! You might hike a trail up a mountain, head to a cliff overlooking the ocean, or perhaps simply take an elevator ride to the top floor of a building downtown. You can also use your binoculars to observe the night sky. Remember, look with your naked eye first and then add binoculars.

OBJECT	WITH YOUR EYES	WITH BINOCULARS
Birds (your own backyard may have ample birds to observe)		
Distant cliffs or hills		
The moon		
River or ocean currents		

OBJECT	WITH YOUR EYES	WITH BINOCULARS
Automobiles (Can you identify the make and model?)		
Animals (Can you name them before and after using the binoculars?)		

— Telescope

If you have the luxury of an observatory in your city, be sure to make use of it! Their telescopes are the most powerful, and you'll be guided by experts who know how to aim them at the most amazing celestial objects. A telescope really drives home how remote most space objects are. It also reminds us that sometimes we have a distorted view of reality because our sight is so limited. Telescopes can help us remember to ask, "What else am I missing?" and "What can't I see right now?" and "What would help me see more than I do currently?"

OBJECT	WITH YOUR EYES	WITH A TELESCOPE
The moon		
Jupiter		
Venus		
Saturn (the rings!)		

OBJECT	WITH YOUR EYES	WITH A TELESCOPE
The Milky Way		
The Perseid meteor shower		
Nebulae		
Star clusters		
The North Star		

JOURNAL

Take a moment to compare your naked-eye observations with those modified by tools of perception. Then reflect on what tools you can use to help you increase your intimacy with a subject matter. How can you get closer to a topic? How can you understand its details? How can you bring something that's far away from your experience closer to you? What can you do to identify details you missed at a glance? As you consider how you can improve your thinking skills, return to the memory of how your perceptions shifted when you took the time to examine the familiar with the aid of a powerful tool that added detail to your perceptions. This workbook is filled with those sorts of activities that you can return to anytime you'd like!

LESSON SIX:

THE ART OF INTERPRETATION

Interpreting Texts Using Critical Thinking

(WORTH REPEATING)

BRIEF

You've reached the most critical part of this workbook: how to interpret a text. Texts are all around you—song lyrics, short videos on social media, billboards, advertisements, books, emails, speeches, poetry, closed captions on streaming services, and literal text messages with their happy face emojis! Each time we read a text, we simultaneously assign meaning to it. For instance, did you know that the phrase "to make love" has changed during the last century? In the early twentieth century, it merely meant "to put the moves on" the person of your infatuation. Today, it has morphed to mean intimate, sexual contact with another person. If you were to read a love letter from 1935 that included that language, you'd want to know what the author meant at the time compared with how you understand that language now! That's an example of how interpretation of texts matters. That's where this lesson's handy questionnaire can help you.

ACTIVITY

Let's get started. To probe deeply into any text you read, it helps to have a series of questions that provoke reflection. You'll want to make notes right on the text as you pose these questions to yourself. You're going to examine the text from two vantage points: the "horizon of the text" (the author's point of view) and the "horizon of the interpreter" (your point of view). After you've completed the interview for each horizon, you'll fuse together those ideas for an original interpretation!

Select a *written* text of about one thousand words for this process. You could choose a novel, poem, speech, historical record or document, religious manuscript, philosophical treatise, textbook, literary criticism, movie review, diary, or newspaper article.

Next, follow these instructions:

1. Print or photocopy the text onto paper with large margins. Shrink the text, if helpful, and allow for two- or three-inch-wide margins. If it's difficult to get the text out of the book for any reason, retype it, triple space it, and print it.

2. In the margins, ask questions of the text. Highlight passages *and* pose questions to the text. Record your true reactions in your natural writing voice. It's perfectly acceptable to write things like, "What on earth does this mean?" or "I can't believe this writer is so ignorant." These first impressions give you a clue about both your bias and what's of interest to you. You may feel confused or provoked. You may agree. Note it all.

3. Underline repeated terms, phrases, evidence, and literary devices. In addition to asking questions about the text, notice writing craft. Does the writer repeat a certain term? Do you know what that term means to both you and the writer? Does the writer include evidence or credible research? Can you trust their sources? Notice the effect of various literary devices, like alliteration or rhyme or assonance. Identify any metaphors or analogies. Put an asterisk next to personal experiences or anecdotes.

4. Correlate your initial observations with other writings or data. The margin notes and questions are a pathway back to the bits of the text that provoked a reaction in you. They can offer an excellent starting place for determining a thesis statement or an angle of focus for a paper. Make connections like "Contrast this idea with Smith's theory in X book" or "Check out this statistic for validity." These kinds of notes help you relocate an important piece of information for further reflection.

After you've read the text and jotted down your questions, highlighted passages, defined a few terms, and made margin notes, it's time to ask yourself some questions. Rereading is critical for this activity. If you choose to use a text longer than one thousand words, scan and look for specific passages to support your answers.

— Horizon of the Interpreter (You)

As you read the text, ask yourself the following questions:

- What do you hope to find in the text?

\
\
\

- What suspicions do you bring to it? Do you read "with" the text or "against" it? In other words, are you a receptive reader or a hostile reader? Simply note which.

\
\
\

- What angers, surprises, and/or relieves you?

\
\
\

Next level:

- What images go with your reading? (See the Part One, Lesson Six: Silent Films questions on page 41 for prompts to probe more deeply.)

_____

_____

- How do you react to the language? Are there stereotypes?

_____

_____

- Do you trust the writer? Why or why not?

_____

_____

- What are your immediate reactions to the writing? (Take a look at your margin notes to help you.)

_____

_____

- What do you wish to avoid? Are there facts or ideas you wish weren't true or didn't come up?

_____

_____

- As you read, what other voices do you reference? Your family? Your religious community? Whose voice is talking to you in your head? A favorite writer? A friend? A leader of some kind?

_____

_____

Next level:

- How does the text relate to your personal experiences?

_____

_____

- Who are you? Does the text affirm your place in the world (your identity, economic status, religious outlook, race, nationality, age group, gender, sexual orientation, education)? Or does it challenge or say nothing to it? Remember, you are multifaceted, so there are several pieces of identity to consider.

_____

_____

_____

- How does the text suggest a hopeful vision? Or does it?

_____

_____

- How does the text suggest doom? Or does it?

_____

_____

_____

- Why are you reading the text? If it's for an assignment, what is the express reason for the assignment? Get at a reason that goes beyond "for class," because usually there is a purpose in the analysis that is meant to engage your critical thinking.

_____

_____

_____

- What is your overall reaction to the text now that you've read it and thought about it a bit?

_____

_____

_____

_____

_____

_____

After you've taken this inventory, it helps to free-write for several minutes. Put your jumble of thoughts into a few free-flowing paragraphs of unedited thought. Then move on to the next inventory.

_____

_____

_____

_____

_____

_____

_____

— Horizon of the Text (Author)

Each piece of writing grows in a specific context. The more recent the publication, the more likely it is that you'll have a firm grasp of the cultural, political, and linguistic world of the text. In most academic settings, however, we're required to examine and comment on writing that is from a remote social, historical, and cultural place. Sometimes you'll even be working with texts translated from other languages, such as a book or a film in another language with subtitles in your own language. Knowing a thing or two about the text's historical, socioeconomic, racial, and political context is critical to accurate readings. Similarly, language and culture impact the writing as well. With these in mind, let's look at how to examine the text/writing itself.

This is a lengthy questionnaire, and not every question needs to be answered. Take it a section at a time during the next week or two. The goal is to stir up new thoughts and ask provocative questions. You'll use what you learn to write *your own interpretation* of the text.

As you reread the text, consider the following:

- What type of text is it—literature, history, criticism, science, religious manuscript, research study, poetry, speech, or news report? The genre (kind) of text helps determine what attitude one takes toward it. If you are working with a legend, you will treat it differently than if you're reading historical records.

_____

_____

- How does the text come to you? Why is it considered important? Who has considered it important?

_____

_____

- What language was it written in? What language are you reading it in? Are there any footnotes that clarify terms or images or references that are unfamiliar to you? Look these up and read them.

_____

_____

Next level:

- How is the text written? Is it meant to be an argument, a narrative, a poem, a record, a political manifesto, or a religious message?

_____

_____

- Is the writing in active or passive voice? Can you identify the narrator (who's telling the story)?

- Is it written for the purpose of entertaining or persuading, warning or reassuring?

- How does the text play on the emotions? Do you notice any particular metaphors, images, or analogies that help the reader "feel" the writer's meaning? Can you identify how they were understood in the original text's era and context? Do they work as well today as they did in the era in which it was written?

- Outline the logic of the piece. What kinds of support does the writer use to make their point? If it's literature, describe the plot line and identify the climax. How does the writer get you there? Does it work?

If it's poetry, what is the ironic moment or the moment of insight? How does the poet get you there? If it's a news report, what are the essential facts, and in what order of significance are they introduced?

_____

_____

_____

_____

Next level:

- Who was the original audience? Were they the intended audience? Was the text commissioned by an authority (the pope, a queen)? Was the writer in danger for writing the text? Did the writer suffer for writing the text?

_____

_____

_____

- How did the original audience receive the text? (For instance, in Shakespeare's day, his plays were well received and notable. Yet some religious texts were completely ignored until years after the writer's death.)

_____

_____

_____

- Was the text meant to consolidate power or subvert it? If it's fiction, does the text address a specific sociopolitical context? Which one and how?

_____

_____

- Are there cultural references that must be understood? What are they? Do you see myths, legends, metaphors, ideas, or motifs in the writing that should be lifted from the text and understood at a deeper level?

_____

_____

Next level:

- What questions does the text attempt to answer? What material from a previous era contributes to these answers?

_____

_____

_____

- What is the historical context? What is the scientific worldview? (Flat earth? Pre-Newtonian? Gods control the weather?) What is the political climate? Who is in power? Does the text support or criticize the prevailing powers?

_____

_____

_____

_____

- How does this text speak to the economic situation of the period?

_____

_____

- What is the situation of the author? Do we know the author's education, genealogy, economic condition, social standing, or reputation at the time of writing and now?

_____

_____

_____

- Has this text come to you with interpretive baggage? Who else has considered it worth interpreting, and how have these previous interpretations influenced your modern reading of the text?

_____

_____

_____

_____

— Fusion of Horizons (You + Author)

It's time to interpret the text! Interpretation is a privilege given to those who care enough to engage the material without making assumptions. It's meant for those who are willing to be transformed by what they read. Interpretation is an art form, and therefore each interpreter's interpretation will bear the marks of unique insight. That means there is no one-size-fits-all interpretation. Yet in many cases, there can be overlapping consensus from a variety of interpreters. The world of academia spends a lot of time debating who has a more compelling reading of a text at any given time, but they realize that multiple readings can offer valid differences in perspective as well.

The art of interpretation is like throwing clay pots or making a crazy quilt or painting a landscape. What you create is an artful rendering of how you now understand the text in question. It will bear the marks of your uniqueness, even as you work to be objective and fair. Interpreting a text is deeply satisfying when you're engaged with patience, curiosity, and care. Answer the following questions in light of the two horizons you've already considered, yours and the writer's. You may not have answers to every question. That's okay!

As you form your interpretation, consider the following:

- What's at stake? That's the crucial question for your entire interpretation. In *Pride and Prejudice*, for instance, the relationship between social convention and personal fulfillment is evaluated and critiqued. What is at stake? The structure of the class system in Britain and the importance of personal choice. Ask yourself what is at stake in this text, story, poem, or document. Also ask what is at stake for readers in this era. How does the text challenge your contemporaries?

_____

_____

_____

_____

- What questions does the text attempt to answer? Which questions can't it answer? Which answers have we found to these questions in the ensuing era, if applicable?

_____

_____

_____

_____

- How does the text move you? What ideas do you find yourself considering? Are they subversive? Are they inspiring? Are they solution-driven or reflection-inducing?

_____

_____

_____

- What subplots or nuances are interesting to you?

_____

_____

_____

- What does the text fail to address?

_____

_____

- How is your worldview or your ideas about reality challenged by the text?

_____

_____

- Summarize what you believe the writer's intended message is.

_____

_____

_____

_____

Next level:

- What prejudices are challenged? What prejudices remain unchallenged?

_____

_____

_____

_____

- How do you think this text influenced its era or spoke to it? How might it speak to ours?

_____

_____

- What community are you a part of, and how does the text relate to it? (This is where you would consider your faith community, nationality, race, economic status, gender, and so on.) Does the text hold an open future for you and your community, or does it subvert it? What loyalties surface for you as you interpret?

_____

_____

_____

- What possibilities are foreclosed (limited) by the message of this text?

_____

_____

- If the writer were on a talk show, what do you think they would want to say to today's audience?

_____

_____

And finally:

- Have you changed during this process of interpretation?

  _____

  _____

- How has your initial hunch or agenda been modified or remained constant?

  _____

  _____

- Have you tried to control your interpretation throughout? Why?

  _____

  _____

  _____

- What is unsaid even after all this work? What more do you wonder?

  _____

  _____

  _____

  _____

— Tentative Conclusions of the Interpreter

After you've gathered your ideas through this guided question format, it's time to take a stab at an initial interpretation. There are a couple of principles to keep in mind.

- You'll write a better interpretation if you sit with your reflections for a few days before you try to synthesize them.

- You're allowed to change your mind. It may be that, when you began, you thought you knew the direction you wanted to take with your response to the text. If the inventory and rereadings have altered that initial hunch, note that. Identify what provoked those changes. Recognizing how a text transforms understanding is a powerful way to form an interpretation.

JOURNAL

The next process is lengthy. You'll learn the most if you give yourself undistracted time to dive deeply into the questions and allow your mind to consider all the possibilities. Once you get going, you may find it quite pleasurable to be able to think that flexibly!

Task of interpretation inventory:

1. Write a narration of what you believe you hear the writer saying, without your point of view. Do your best to remove any judgmental language, any time-bound assumptions, and any of your own ideas. Stick to what you believe the author is saying, even if you disagree with the writer.

2. Write about your relationship to the text, looking for places of connection (experiences, ideals, compatible images, anecdotes, and analogies).

3. Review your responses in the "Fusion of Horizons (You + Author)" section. Identify the compelling idea that has emerged. Write about it with support from the original text while addressing the unique context in which the text is being read today.

4. Check your interpretation against those of other interpreters.

ACCOUNT FOR EVERYONE

Problem-Solving by Including as Many Perspectives as Possible

(WORTH REPEATING)

BRIEF

Have you ever thought you knew how someone else felt in the world, only to one day discover that you actually didn't understand their experience at all? That happened to me when I broke my ankle. Until that time, I thought that most people who used wheelchairs had adequate access to places of business, sports stadiums, concert halls, and gas station bathrooms. I used a wheelchair for six months, and suddenly my eyes were opened! Even though wheelchair access is a legal requirement for businesses, the amount of space dedicated to ease of movement varies wildly. Being in a wheelchair is routinely frustrating. I had no idea! I gained brand-new compassion for people I thought I had understood before.

One of the key challenges to thinking well is that we make the assumption that we know how it is for someone else. When confronted with a tricky issue that needs resolution, most of us move toward "conversion." We become passionate about getting the other person to fully align with our "better" way of seeing the issue.

Unfortunately, when we focus on conversion, we forget that the other person may have particular experiences that need to be accounted for in our solutions. One researcher, Iris Marion Young, reminds us to embrace a stance of "asymmetrical reciprocity." This multisyllable phrase simply means to recognize just how fundamentally different we are from one another. We begin with wonder: being curious about how someone else shows up in the world before assuming we know how it is. For instance, if you want to discuss a social issue like how we manage guns in our free society, before you begin with a strategy of conversion (winning someone over to "your" side), it's helpful to step back and wonder how this topic impacts the other person. It helps to recognize that the other person's experience is meaningful and also unknowable to you. When we look at complex issues, solutions are best achieved when we account for as many perspectives as possible.

ACTIVITY

In this activity, you will address two kinds of complex issues. The first will be an issue that routinely occurs in your family. The second will be a social issue that matters to you.

— Family Matter

Name an issue that needs solving in your family. Typical issues include who gets control of the television; how computer time gets allocated; or who does household chores like laundry, lawn mowing, vacuuming, or making dinner and cleaning up.

Issue to solve:

_____

Interview each person who is impacted by the issue. You want to understand what their needs are and why they feel entitled to the solution that would work best for them. For example, you might have four siblings who all want time on one computer. Each person will have a time allotment and time of day in mind and an idea of what's fair. Jot down the ideal scenario for each person.

- Person one:

_____

- Person two:

_____

- Person three:

  _____

- Person four:

  _____

- Your own thoughts:

  _____

Next, take some time to think about each of the competing needs. Brainstorm as many solutions as you can that take as many of the needs into account as possible. You might find only one solution, or you may find several. No matter what, do everything you can to include each person's specific needs in your solution. (This is not easy and may take you a day or more of mulling things over to come up with a quality idea.)

— Social Issue

This time, pick a social issue that matters to you.

Select one of these typical issues that are hot topics in the United States:

- Gun control/rights
- Abortion
- Death penalty
- Gay marriage
- Teaching Black history

- Books selected for public education
- Gender transition for minors
- Affirmative action in colleges

- Tax exemption for religious property
- Or an issue of your own choosing

Social issue:

_____

First, let's call up your position and identify your loyalties.

- What's at stake?

_____

- What would you have to give up to change your mind?

_____

- Who would be disappointed in you if you did change your mind?

_____

- What values do you fear you'd have to betray to be fair to this topic?

_____

- Who are the sources of authority in your community? How do they see this topic?

_____

_____

- How would your community see you if you changed your mind? Would your membership be at risk?

_____

_____

_____

- Who are the people who hold a different perspective than yours? Do you see them as friends, enemies, or neutral parties?

_____

_____

- What practices in your life are associated with your current view?

_____

_____

- What practices would you have to change if you adopted this other viewpoint?

_____

_____

_____

- How are these ideas in conflict with the community logic stories you've been taught?

_____

_____

_____

_____

Next, you'll want to find two or three people who are invested in this topic and have different experiences from yours. You may have to rely on online reports from people who hold additional perspectives if you don't personally know anyone.

Ask these questions to each person who has a different related experience:

- How do you characterize your viewpoint as moral or justifiable?

_____

_____

- What logic story drives your viewpoint?

_____

_____

- What hunch is at work in your perspective? (Remember, a hunch is the belief that if people adopted that person's viewpoint, the world would be a better place.)

_____

_____

_____

- How does your community see my community? Friends, enemies, or neutral parties?

_____

_____

- What practices characterize your community? Do these practices have social value or personal meaning?

_____

_____

- Who are the sources of authority in your community? How does your community see my community's sources of authority? How did your community form those views?

_____

_____

JOURNAL

Imagine as many possible solutions as you can to your topic. As you consider each one, ask who is included in the solution and whose needs or particular experiences are not being addressed. See if you can account for as many viewpoints as possible.

Here's an example: Picture a group of tenth-grade students, and consider how they might respond to these questions on the issue of gun control/rights:

- What is meant by the concept of "regulation" in the Second Amendment ("a well-regulated militia")? Are we regulating people, guns, or both?

- How much regulation should the government be empowered to have? Should that control be federal or by state?

- Background checks: What kind are appropriate?

- Waiting periods for purchasing guns: How long should they be, if they exist at all?

- Right to purchase: Who can own a gun? Adults? Children? What about people who have been convicted of crimes?

- Varieties of guns: Which types can be purchased? Any restrictions at all?

- Regulations for use: Open or concealed carry? "Stand your ground" laws that protect armed citizens who shoot when they feel under attack, or no?

Imagine one student comes from a family in which a sibling has been killed in a school shooting. Someone else has a parent who teaches in a school with active shooter drills. Another student comes from a family with generations of hunters. Perhaps another teen has a parent who is a police officer, and someone else has a parent who is in the military. Maybe another family has a tragic story of an accidental gun death, where the firearm went off without anyone intending it to. Each of these perspectives (and others) will shape the solutions proposed for how to address the role guns play in the United States. When journaling possible solutions, how many of these perspectives can you account for in one comprehensive solution?

As you consider the topic of your choice, look for a set of questions you can ask about the topic and then identify as many possible experiences in the population as you can. Get to know their perspectives, and journal about what the various needs are. If you feel creative and brave, propose a solution that accounts for as many of the positions as you can.

The key to this activity is accepting that radical difference is meant to be both respected and accounted for, rather than converted to a single understanding.

_____

_____

_____

_____

_____

_____

_____

THE BELIEVING GAME

Flipping the Script from Doubt to Belief

(WORTH REPEATING)

BRIEF

You've examined so many viewpoints in this workbook, giving patient consideration to the way you think and how you're influenced by the thinking of others. Let's flip that experience on its head for this activity. Instead of examining your own thoughts, challenge yourself to sit inside a perspective you don't hold. My favorite writing coach, Dr. Peter Elbow, calls this practice the "believing game." All of us are good at the doubting game. It's the primary tool of science as well as literary and historical criticism. (The word "criticism" is baked right into the latter two disciplines!) Doubting is a powerful academic tool that has resulted in massive advances in every field—from science to technology to medicine to the social sciences. The danger of leaning heavily on our doubts whenever we hear a point of view we don't hold is that we sometimes miss an important feature of that perspective that would help us become more nuanced thinkers—or even reconsider our own stereotypes or poorly vetted perspectives. The believing game asks you to "pretend" that you hold an alternative belief by listening without defending your own position. It's a chance to inhabit a view you don't hold as though you do. This is taking the stance of "wonder" and "accepting radical difference" to the next level—a kind of Jedi Master level of thinking!

Remember how we talked about the idea that an actor can create a character who has beliefs and ideas that the actor doesn't hold? That's a little bit of the feeling you want to create in this activity. Pretend you hold the belief, and see what information you need to rely on to support the position. Give yourself the best chance to adopt the views of the opposing side for a moment to see what you learn. (Don't worry; you can scurry back to your beloved viewpoint when you finish.)

ACTIVITY

This next activity is provocative. You're going to give your mind a task: to find support for a position you don't hold. If you get annoyed while engaged in research, that's a good sign you're on the right track.

1. Choose a controversial issue. The scale is less important than how committed you are to your position. Try picking a topic that you feel strongly about first. For instance, perhaps you feel strongly that violent video games are not dangerous for teenagers to play. Now, choose to adopt the counter position: that violent video games do impact teens adversely and may contribute to violent outbursts.

2. Your task will be to hunt down support for your adopted position—to qualify the evidence, to deliberately look for information that backs up this position you don't hold but that you are pretending to hold. Discount the support for your *actual* position, if you stumble onto it. Instead, look for as many reasons as you can to support the idea that video games are dangerous to a teen's imagination (or whatever topic you choose).

   • What topic will you use for the believing game?

   _____

   • What position do you hold now?

   _____

   • What position will you "believe" or pretend to hold?

   _____

- List the titles of articles you find that support the opposing view.

_____

_____

_____

_____

- List the key arguments you are "believing."

_____

_____

_____

_____

- List the authoritative sources for those arguments and why they can be trusted, according to a person who holds this position. For instance, you may not be religious, but a religious person might find a trusted religious leader's perspective compelling and authoritative. Include both the reasons and the source.

_____

_____

_____

_____

_____

_____

- List the counterarguments that someone holding this position might use in response to the opposing side. (This means finding all the reasons to discredit the position you *actually* hold.)

_____

_____

_____

_____

_____

- What metaphors or images come to mind when you do this work of imagining holding this perspective?

_____

_____

_____

_____

- What's at stake for people who hold this view? (For instance, someone against violent video games may be concerned about safety from shootings in schools and is associating video game play with mass shootings.)

_____

_____

_____

_____

_____

JOURNAL

Begin by writing a summary of the view you chose to "believe." See if you can run it by someone who holds that view. How close did you come to representing it accurately without your own judgment sneaking into the description? By believing the opposing view, even for a little while, you likely came across some surprises in your research. What were they? How do they impact the view you do hold? Did they strengthen your position or cause you to reconsider something? Did you feel you were betraying anyone by reading the other side so openly? If so, who and why? How has your understanding of the topic grown? If you were to talk about this topic with someone today, what new aspects of the topic would you include in your discussion? Did you discover any ways that the other side misunderstands the position you do hold? What were they?

_____

_____

_____

THE COURAGE TO CHANGE YOUR MIND

Being Brave about What You Believe

(WORTH REPEATING)

BRIEF

Well done! You're nearly at the end of a hardworking critical-thinking journey through this workbook. Is your brain fried? Mine is! It takes work to think well. It also takes courage. The most powerful tool you can take with you into adulthood is the courage to change your mind. In fact, you'll surprise your friends and sometimes even dazzle your family when you do. "Yeah, I used to think X, but after learning Y, I shifted my position to Z." When you change your mind, you give others permission to do the same. The biggest hurdle most people face when confronted with facts or information they don't want to be true (but, in fact, is valid!) is the embarrassment of *changing their minds*. Changing your mind can feel like betrayal of your best friends, a failure of previous thinking, and the mortification of remembering all the times you trumpeted your beliefs without considering any other perspective. But the more of us who show flexibility in our beliefs—learning, modifying, and growing—the more we invite others to grow and change, too.

You see, now you know how to vet sources for credibility. You know how to measure statistics against their benchmarks. You understand how big a role your community loyalty and personal identity play in determining which beliefs you hold.

You've learned how to examine your assumptions as well as those of your opponents. You've discovered that some of your beliefs need a fresh look or recalibration. As a result, you can overturn a previously strongly held belief because you can't unsee new information that alters how you understand the issues.

Changing your mind doesn't necessarily mean abandoning your original position. It simply may mean taking into account additional factors or stories—adding a new angle to your view or creating a more precise description of what your view is. You might realize that the people who disagree with you have good reasons for their fears or worries. You might discover that you need to reexamine your solutions to account for what those other people need to feel protected or included as well.

It takes courage to change your mind because you put your familiar relationships at risk. People like agreement a lot. They are willing to lose family and friends to retain their feeling of belonging to a community of like-minded people. So in the privacy of this workbook, away from any risk at all, let's take a look at how you've been impacted by everything you've learned as you worked through the lessons.

ACTIVITY

You may or may not have changed your mind about a particular issue while doing the activities in this workbook. The best place to land at the end of this journey is to recognize what is at stake when you *do* feel a craving to change your mind. I remember when I was considering significant changes in a few of my beliefs, and I reached out to my aunt, who was a university professor. I knew she would be able to hear me without judgment and give me excellent support and feedback while I was in crisis. I want that for you, too. Take this inventory to prepare yourself for the moment when you consider changing your mind about any issue that matters to you:

1. If I change my mind about _____, what's at stake?

    _____

2. Which community would support me in that change? Do I know anyone in it?

    _____

3. Who can be my confidant and friend when I examine a belief that is especially important to my family, friends, religious community, or social group?

_____

4. Write about a belief you are currently reexamining. What caused you to reconsider your belief? What can you do to be supportive of yourself as you look into it more?

_____

_____

JOURNAL

Use the following page to describe the impact of your work during the last several weeks. What have you learned about critical thinking? Review your definitions of the critical thinking terms from Part One, Lesson Three: Fab Vocab Quick-Write. Have any of your ideas about those words changed or deepened? What's one concept that has meant a lot to you? How has it impacted how you read or think about to-day's issues? Remember, any idea you consider can be reconsidered many times. You also have the right not to declare any position. It's okay to not know, to want more information, or to wait to see how you feel about an idea after sitting with it for a while. In the end, you have the ability to think well, and to think again.

_____

_____

_____

_____

OPEN ARTIFICIAL INTELLIGENCE

Making AI Work for You

(WORTH REPEATING)

BRIEF

You've come to the end of this workbook. Well done! Give yourself a high-five and then, if you dare, I've got one more exercise for you—related to the mysterious world of artificial intelligence (AI) and how it's impacting you as a student.

Today, our thinking faculties are being challenged in more ways than ever! With the advent of AI through ChatGPT (software that generates writing that is believably close to a human's writing voice), machine learning, and deepfakes (videos that are altered to manipulate one person's likeness to appear like another), it's getting more and more difficult to sort information pushed onto our screens as fact versus misinformation. Our task is to carry a healthy skepticism when we encounter any unsourced material. We can ask, "Says who?" We can apply the CACAO rubric (currency, accuracy, coverage, authority, objectivity) to ensure that the information we pass along is accurate. It's easy to scare up reasons to resist these technological advances. The truth is, they're likely here to stay. It's important to learn to use them well rather than to slip into a cave and hide.

As it turns out, ChatGPT can be quite useful to students. It enables you to discover a narrative explanation for any topic of interest, it can create tables and graphs of details you supply at a far quicker rate than you can construct them, and it offers you a chance to hear the cadence of a particular writing style before you attempt it for yourself—to name a few of the ways it can support your education. The key to using any new powerful technology is to stay curious and cautiously optimistic. (At least, that's my opinion!) ChatGPT is unlikely to be a problem in your education if you use it as a tool to help you grow your writing and thinking skills rather than as a do-it-for-you tool you use to excuse yourself from writing and thinking. For now, let's play with it! It's really fun to watch the program populate fields with words in real time. Then I've got a few questions for you to consider as you think about the role ChatGPT may play in public discourse and education.

ACTIVITY

In this activity, your task is to explore ChatGPT to see what it can do. You'll find it at chat.openai.com. Once you create an account, try these activities. You'll get a chance to vet some of the sources it offers you. There are no right answers in this activity. Rather, the goal is to discover the possible ways you might use ChatGPT in your development as a writer and thinker.

Try these:

1. Ask ChatGPT how it can help you with whichever project you are writing now. For instance, you might ask it for assistance with a question like "What are primary themes I can explore in the play *Romeo and Juliet*?" You'll be guided to consider a few suggested themes, the same way you might be guided by a book in the library or an article in an academic journal. The difference with ChatGPT is that the information will be distilled into an answer that specifically addresses your question. No hunting through an index or chapter titles. No scrolling through a list of website links. When I posed the above question in the "new chat" window on ChatGPT, I received a list of possible themes to explore: love, fate and destiny, conflict, youth and impulsiveness, appearance versus reality, gender roles, and light and dark imagery. These suggestions serve as prompts for deeper investigation of the text.

What topic would you like to explore?

_____

What did ChatGPT suggest?

_____

_____

Do you find the suggestions useful? Why or why not?

_____

2. Pick a style of poetry—ballad, sonnet, limerick, etc. Now pick a topic—any interest you have, like reading, playing a sport, or travel. Put the topic into the "new chat" space. Include specific details that are meaningful to you about that interest. Ask ChatGPT to write a poem in your chosen style for your chosen topic. At the bottom of the newly created poem, you'll see another prompt: "Regenerate response?" Click that, and watch ChatGPT write another poem in that style using the same topic. Try it again! When you have three poems, analyze them to determine how they were built. What rhyme scheme is used? What meter (how many beats per line)? How are they similar and different? Do you prefer one to another? Why? Try writing a similar poem in that format for a different topic without the aid of ChatGPT but using the three poems as models to follow. What did you learn in this process?

_____

_____

_____

_____

_____

_____

3. Select a topic or concept that you struggle to understand. Perhaps you pick a grammar concept like "past participle" or a specific term from a current field of study like "algorithm" from computer programming. Jot down the term and a quick definition based on your current understanding.

_____

Enter that term in the "new chat" space with a request for ChatGPT to give you an explanation of its meaning. What definition did it give?

_____

_____

_____

What did you learn? Did the explanation help? How did it complement or differentiate itself from your understanding? (Remember, we did this activity in Part One, Lesson Three: Fab Vocab Quick-Write. Now you're including AI in your definition search.)

_____

_____

_____

4. When you find yourself struggling to think through another side of an argument you know well, ChatGPT can give you a dispassionate take to help you scale back your reactivity. Think about the debated ideas you've investigated in this workbook so far. Select a topic you've already explored, such as video games and violence, gun control/rights, abortion, the US Electoral College, the legal limit for driving under the influence, animal rights, marriage rights, or a topic of your own choosing. Write the topic and your position here:

_____

_____

_____

_____

Now describe how you understand the other side, without revealing any bias for your own position as you write it:

_____

_____

_____

Ask ChatGPT to provide you with an argument for the other side. Jot that here:

_____

_____

_____

Compare your answer to the one you got from ChatGPT. How did the AI response help you expand your own point of view? How did it surprise you? Did it help you uncover any of your own bias?

_____

_____

_____

_____

What else do you notice? For instance, how does it feel when you can read the other side's perspective without attaching it to a specific writer, thinker, or person in your life? Are you more able to read the information without reacting? Do you trust the information? What else do you notice?

_____

_____

5. Creative writing can be aided by AI as well. Ask ChatGPT to provide you with writing prompts for your age ("Provide me with writing prompts for a sixteen-year-old") and then pick one. Write your response here:

_____

_____

_____

You also can be wildly specific: "Give me a writing prompt that uses these three items" or "Teach me how to write fantasy. Provide writing prompts to help me." See what happens when you use ChatGPT as a tutor, not just an answer-giver.

Jot down a few of the prompts below. Using a separate sheet of paper, try free-writing to one of the prompts.

_____

_____

6. ChatGPT can also provide support with grammar and the polishing of a piece of writing. You can use ChatGPT to help you identify a better way to express an idea or to ensure accuracy in spelling, punctuation, and grammar. You can follow up by asking for an explanation of the changes it made so that you learn more about your writing habits. Enter a rough draft text now; you might use the free-writing from the preceding step. Ask ChatGPT to edit it and then explain its edits. What did you learn?

_____

_____

7. Another way to use this technology is to ask it to give you step-by-step instructions for an activity you know well (pickleball, Wii bowling, the Suzuki method for the violin, doing the backstroke, caring for ferrets, throwing clay pots, and so on). Compare what AI generates with your experience. Did you learn anything new? Did it omit any essential steps? Now try asking for step-by-step instructions for an activity you don't know well. See if you can follow them and get a good result. What do you think of ChatGPT's ability to provide instructions or directions?

_____

_____

_____

JOURNAL

Artificial intelligence is here to stay. It harms us if people allow it to be a substitute rather than a tool for learning. One of the dangers with the current iteration of AI and writing generators is that sources for data are not always included. It's important to keep your commitment to vetting the information it gives for accuracy. There was a time when calculators were seen as dangerous to students, preventing them from doing the hard work of calculating math problems in their minds. Today, we use calculators of all kinds to help us do advanced mathematics quickly. Computers have given us the ability to be far more mathematically capable as a human population. They support the advancement of math; they haven't prevented mathematical breakthroughs. Consider how Photoshop and other graphic design programs have expanded the ways artists create and maximize their output.

Could ChatGPT become a supportive tool in the field of research and writing? That's the nagging question experts are now considering. Does a tool like ChatGPT make us lazy, replacing the harder work of thinking for ourselves? Might ChatGPT put copywriters and customer service specialists out of work? Will ChatGPT and other AI tools mask student aptitude, if students grow accustomed to relying on AI rather than developing their own skills for thinking and writing?

Use this space to consider ways AI may serve us going forward and ways it might be dangerous or damaging. You might even ask ChatGPT the same question after you jot down your own thoughts to see what it says about itself! Also consider asking ChatGPT how it generates writing, how it supplies data, and how it sorts and vets information. Then do an online search for articles that explain the mechanisms and algorithms that enable ChatGPT to function. Compare the two, and consider what you learned. Can you think of any other reasons to be cautious and/or optimistic about AI's role in learning in the future?

_____

_____

_____

_____

CONGRATULATIONS!

What a journey you've been on! How's your head holding up? It's a lot of work to examine your thinking and that of others. It's the main reason so few adults like to do it! Most of us find it easier to live in an echo chamber of our own ideas among friends and family who agree with us. The choice to become a skillful thinker, however, gives you superpowers. Some of those powers include curiosity, clarity, compassion, concern for accuracy, competence, and conviction. When you find it difficult to *know* what's true, you can be curious. When you don't *know*, you can be clear about that as well! You can remember that other people are also busy constructing reality to make it make sense to them, just like you do. You can ask for a source or vet a statistic to be sure it holds up. You can grow your capacity to listen to arguments for and against hot-button topics. And you can stand with conviction on the beliefs you develop because you'll know you've put in the hard work of thinking all the way through a topic. Even then, you can hold those beliefs with humility, knowing that new information or data can impact what you *know* to be true.

If you got to the end of this workbook and realize that you know less now than when you started, congratulations! Critical thinking often feels like walking into bigger and bigger rooms as you let the sunlight of new ideas and additional factors impact how you think. You may notice that you are more interested in identifying what else matters in a conversation than merely restating your own position again and again. When you notice that you have made that shift, you'll know that your own mind has expanded. That's a great day!

For now, take a nice long break. You deserve time off to play, rest, and chill out. The mind likes time off as much as it likes thinking. Be sure to do both for a balanced, happy, healthy life. Then come back and change the world. Please? Thanks in advance.

ABOUT THE AUTHOR

JULIE BOGART is the creator of the award-winning, innovative Brave Writer program, teaching writing and language arts to thousands of families for more than twenty-five years. She's the founder of Brave Learner Home, a 15,000-member community that supports homeschooling parents through coaching and teaching. She is also the host of the popular *Brave Writer* podcast. Bogart holds a BA from UCLA and an MA from Xavier University, where she's taught as an adjunct professor and was awarded the prestigious Madges Award for Outstanding Contribution to Society. She has five adult kids and three grandchildren. Bogart is also the author of *The Brave Learner* and *Raising Critical Thinkers*.